CHRISTIAN
MISSION:

THE STEWARDSHIP OF
LIFE

IN THE KINGDOM OF
DEATH

CHRISTIAN MISSION:

THE STEWARDSHIP OF LIFE

IN THE KINGDOM OF DEATH

by
Douglas John Hall

Friendship Press • New York
for
Commission on Stewardship
National Council of the Churches of Christ in the U.S.A.

LIBRARY OF CHRISTIAN STEWARDSHIP

Handbook of Stewardship Procedures
    T.K. Thompson
Stewardship in Mission
    Winburn T. Thomas
The Christian Meaning of Money
    Otto A. Piper
Stewardship Illustrations
    T.K. Thompson
Why People Give
    Martin E. Carlson
Punctured Preconceptions
    Douglas W. Johnson and
    George W. Cornell
The Steward: A Biblical Symbol Come of Age
    Douglas John Hall
Teaching and Preaching Stewardship—An Anthology
    Nordan C. Murphy, editor
Christian Mission: The Stewardship of Life
    in the Kingdom of Death
    Douglas John Hall

ISBN 0-377-00156-2

COVER DESIGN
E. Paul Lansdale

Dedicated
with gratitude and affection
to

John Coleman Bennett,

Mentor

September 1st, 1939

Defenceless under the night
Our world in stupor lies;
Yet, dotted everywhere,
Ironic points of light
Flash out wherever the Just
Exchange their messages:
May I, composed like them
Of Eros and of dust,
beleagured by the same
Negation and despair,
Show an affirming flame.

—*W.H. Auden*

"One reason why the churches have not helped the laity to see the Christian significance of their vocation in the world is that the churches had lost sight of the cosmic dimension of the gospel. This could only lead to self-centered ecclesiasticism or pietism. When we realize again that Christ is the *hope of the world*, we see also that activity in the world is meaningful. It does not carry its meaning within itself, but it has a goal, an end: the kingdom. Christians are men and women who live toward that future and manifest this faith by acts which express their hope and expectation. At a time when—because of the collapse of the doctrine of progress—there is a great danger that all human effort is poisoned by a sense of futility, the Church has the great opportunity of re-creating a sense of the meaningfulness and worthwhileness of worldly vocation."

—*W.A. Visser't Hooft*

TABLE OF CONTENTS

FOREWORD iii

FIRST MEDITATION: "THY KINGDOM COME . . . ON EARTH"   1
Introduction: Christian Mission in Confusion
1 Our Heritage: Conquering for Christ
2 A Different Perspective
3 What Is Our Mission, Then?
4 The Harvest Is Plentiful
5 "Go Your Way—I Send You Out"
6 The Kingdom of God Has Come Near To You
7 The "Religious" Rejection of God's Kingdom
8 Mission Does Not Mean Expansion
9 Thy Kingdom Come . . . On Earth

DIALOGUE   22

SECOND MEDITATION: THE CONTEXT OF OUR MISSION:
                                  A COVENANT WITH DEATH   29
1 Bargaining with Death
2 The Death of the Spirit
3 The Religion of Death Behind the Politics of Death
4 For Want of a Vision

DIALOGUE   41

THIRD MEDITATION: THE BASIS OF OUR MISSION:
                              GOD's COVENANT WITH LIFE   46
1 For Love of the World
2 "Whither Thou Wouldst Not"
3 On Swimming Against the Stream
4 Spelling Out God's Covenant With Life

DIALOGUE   60

FOURTH MEDITATION: THE MANDATE OF OUR MISSION:
                                   STEWARDSHIP OF LIFE   68
Introduction and Recapitulation
1 The Gospel: Life is There for the Choosing
2 The Law Within the Gospel

3 Courage to Choose
4 When Choice Becomes Necessity
5 "Jesus Christ, the Life of the World"

DIALOGUE   81

FIFTH MEDITATION: THE GOAL OF OUR MISSION:
                   ABUNDANT LIFE   87
1 The Spiritualization of the Christian Message
2 The Other Side of the Coin: Christian Worldliness
3 Life as Process and as Vision
4 Life as a Revolution of Hope
Conclusion

DIALOGUE   101

AFTERWORD   107

END NOTES   108

FOREWORD

This is a book about the Christian mission in our time, our place. I do not presume to speak for every time and place, but I do want to speak for ours. In our time and place, I believe, it is necessary to define the Christian mission in terms of life and death. To engage in Christ's mission in the world today is to be stewards of life in the kingdom of death.

Since I wrote *The Steward: A Biblical Symbol Come of Age*, in relation to which this present book is a kind of sequel, two things have become clearer to me. The first is that we are living in a context that can legitimately be named a "Kingdom of Death." The second is that the Gospel of Jesus as the Christ is at the most rudimentary level an affirmation of life. The two realizations are obviously interrelated.

It is too strong, too one-sided to characterize our time and place as "The Kingdom of Death"? I don't think so. As I sit here at my typewriter composing this sentence, six millions of Ethiopians are starving to death; death-squads in various Latin and Central American nations are hunting down rebels, most of whom are driven to rebel by some life-affirming doctrine or impulse; victims of Hiroshima and Nagasaki, in the presence of one of whom, just last night, I felt a sense of inextinguishable shame, are living witnesses to the fact that the death-dealing powers of our world do not emanate solely from sources *outside* our context; millions of persons in the First and Second worlds are expending their best intellectual and physical energies perfecting and tending the engines of death that are poised for instant deployment against every major city on both sides of the tragic curtain. . . .

One could go on. In what follows I shall go on. We *must* go on, we Christians and all others who are committed to life, go on naming death as it stalks our world, because to be silent is to sanction it. To continue using the bland and polite language of liberal religion, always balancing our negative statements with positive ones, and so creating the impression that the life of the world is indeed a well-balanced affair is to betray the truth of God and to contribute to the multifold disaster that humankind is courting. When even the scientific community can talk of the proximity of doomsday, are we theologians and preachers so congenitally bound to the niceties of academe and the sweetness of suburbia that we are incapable of calling a spade a spade? One of the great boons of the Christian tradition is that it offers us a wealth of words and categories, metaphors, concepts and symbols for naming the realities that destroy God's beloved world and negate our hope. We call ourselves the people of the cross. *The Cross!* Yet all too often we are hesitant to come anywhere near the environs of Golgotha. Perhaps that is why our prescriptions for life seem so insipid, so lacking in conviction and color, just more of the same thing that our congretations already enjoy.

It is not accidental that the little group huddled around the cross of Calvary only began to remember that Jesus was "the *life* of the world" as they pondered the meaning of that bleak death. Coming into close proximity with death can do that for one, even under less dramatic circumstances. We don't know what we're missing until we realize that it can be taken away from us. We don't ask whether we've tasted it fully until we're shown that it's not going to be there for the tasting forever. There are more reasons than one why "the Son of man had to suffer. . . ."

In the face of the manifold forms of death our world is flirting with, Christians could, I think, begin to understand more deeply that our gospel is about life. When I first heard the theme of the World Council of Churches' meeting in Vancouver I thought to myself, "Ho, hum. What else would it be!" But consciously or unconsciously, the planners of the Council chose precisely the right words: "Jesus Christ, the Life of the World." I am not in a position to judge whether the Council explored the profundity of its own motto, but the words were right.

But both nouns in the phrase Life of the World have to be stressed. The gospel is an affirmation of life, but not just life-in-general, or in the abstract, but the life *of the world.* To hear this gospel under *any* circumstances is to be enlisted as a participant in God's struggle to save the life of God's world. But to hear it under circumstances like ours, where death is being teased and beckoned in high places and low, is to find oneself at the center of what is quite literally a *life-and-death* struggle.

In such a context, the ancient concept of stewardship is lifted clear out of its rather innocuous, domesticated past. It becomes an all-encompassing symbol for the meaning of the Christian life, as I said in *The Steward.* Now I want to say more than that. Stewardship in the Kingdom of Death connotes a *strategy*, a plan of action, a style of confrontation, a resistance and a protest that is at the same time the presentation of a radical alternative. It is not only money and time and talents of which we are stewards now. It is not only nature and human resources and the other creatures, either. It is more inclusive than all these things. *It is life itself.* We are called and commanded to be stewards of life, and to be this in an environment that is perhaps more hostile to such a calling, and certainly more skeptical of it, than ever before in history. The stewarding of life in a context reeking of death: that *is*, today, our Christian mission. It may not be the way that Christians four generations hence will want to express their mission. In a real sense, I hope that it is not. But when the very life of creation is threatened, there is no other appropriate way of discussing the matter.

+ + + + + +

I have written these five chapters in the form of meditations. All the texts on which they are based, save the first, are from the older Testament, though I have tried throughout to relate them concretely to the basic motifs of the newer Testament. That I have chosen passages from the Hebrew Bible may be taken as indicative of my belief that the newer Testament only communicates to us what it means to communicate when it is seen in continuity with the Hebraic scriptures, particularly in connection with a theme like the present one. It is far too easy for Christians to spiritualize both of the basic terms of these meditations, particularly the term "life," unless they reflect on them in the presence of the earthy faith of Israel.

While the meditations are grounded in Scripture, however, they are not intended in any way as detailed scholarly exegesis of the passages in question. What I have wanted to explore in the scriptural passages that I have used is the metaphor, the central motif they present. I hope my interpretations of these passages are not *un*scholarly; but my purpose is quite different from the verse-by-verse exposition that would normally be undertaken by the biblical exegete.

The meditations were developed over a period of almost two years, and in connection with public lectures that I had been asked to give, largely in the United States. In varying forms, they have been used in centers all across the continent—New York, Detroit, Madison, Chicago, Sacramento, Portland, Boise, etc. As I explored these themes with Presbyterian, Lutheran, Methodist, Church of the Brethren, Baptist, United Church of Christ, United Church of Canada, Anglican/Episcopalian and other audiences, I received a great variety of responses. Most of them, I am glad to be able to say, were positive and constructive, and some were intensely thought-provoking. In the various stages of the reworking of the manuscript, these responses have greatly influenced my work. I can legitimately consider this a work of corporate theology. Readers who were present at any of these sessions may well recognize themselves in some of these pages.

They may also recognize their explicit question in the brief sections that I have included after each meditation, under the heading, *Dialogue*. For some of the questions that I heard were so useful, and some were so often stated, that I felt they should be included here and responded to explicitly, rather than simply woven into the text along with other, more general concerns expressed by my hearers. It was in my mind that these dialogues following each of the five meditations could be especially useful where the book is used for group study purposes.

I am greatly indebted to the National Council of Churches' Commission on Stewardship, and in particular to Dr. Nordan Murphy, for the invitation to present such a sequel to my earlier book for them. Nordan Murphy has been a constant source of encouragement to me, not only because he has responded so warmly to my modest efforts to evolve a theology of stewardship, but because he is himself such an exemplary model of the Christian steward.

I am also grateful to the hundreds of men and women, clergy and lay persons, who have heard these meditations in their evolving forms, and whose intense and dedicated interest in the themes here presented is the most hopeful thing I have found in our society. Finally, I express my unending gratitude to Rhoda, my wife, who carefully read the manuscript, and whose discourse is the *sine qua non* of all my thought and life.

—*Douglas John Hall*

Faculty of Religious Studies,
McGill University,
Montreal, Canada
November, 1984

"THY KINGDOM COME .... ON EARTH"

... The Lord appointed seventy others and sent them on ahead of him, two by two, into every town and place where he himself was about to come. And he said to them, 'The harvest is plentiful, but the laborers are few; pray, therefore, the Lord of the harvest to send out laborers into his harvest. Go your way; behold, I send you out as lambs in the midst of wolves. Carry no purse, no bag, no sandals; and salute no one on the road. Whatever house you enter, first say, 'Peace be to this house!' And if a son of peace is there, your peace shall rest upon him; but if not, it shall return to you. And remain in the same house, eating and drinking what they provide, for the laborer deserves his wages; do not go from house to house. Whenever you enter a town and they receive you, eat what is set before you; heal the sick in it and say to them, 'The kingdom of God has come near to you.' But whenever you enter a town and they do not receive you, go into its streets and say, 'Even the dust of your town that clings to our feet, we wipe off against you; nevertheless know this, that the kingdom of God has come near.' I tell you it shall be more tolerable on that day for Sodom than for that town.'

—Luke 10: 1–12

Introduction: Christian Mission in Confusion

A puzzling and somewhat ironic situation exists within Christendom today. Those forms of the church that used to be peripheral—so far off center, some of them, as to have earned the epithet "the lunatic fringe"—have sprung to the forefront. They are full of vim and vigor; they dominate the media and the mentality of the general public; they do not lack for material support; above all, they have a very definite and confident sense of their Christian mission. Meanwhile, the older, established churches that in the recent past constituted that dominant and normative center in relation to which these others could be

1

thought peripheral and sectarian have languished. They have suffered quantitative and qualitative losses and seem uncertain not only what they are in themselves but also what they ought to be doing in the world.

The ironic twist in this situation is evident to anyone familiar with recent ecclesiastical history. For it was precisely the old, mainline denominations that invented the modern version of Christian mission as a universal undertaking; and now the very sectarian elements they deemed unworthy of global attention have overtaken them in spectacular ways, while they appear disenchanted and perhaps destined for an even greater humiliation than their present state.

Is this a classic case of the underdog making good, the downtrodden becoming successful, the last being first and the first last? What has been going on in the world and the church to bring about this situation? What sense, if any, can be made of it? More important, what good might come of it?

I shall not attempt here to explain the rise of sectarian Christianity to prominence on the North American continent. It is a complex story, and by no means based on wholly religious themes. My basic concern is with the fate of the older forms of the church. It seems to me all too clear that the remnants of classical Protestantism on this continent are in trouble. At the same time, I have never felt so strongly as I now do that there is a significant role within our present sociological context for what classical Protestantism at its best stood for. Providence is offering us a way out of the doldrums, a way of becoming not big or important or successful, but faithful! We could become a significant witnessing community at a time of profound need in the affairs of peoples and nations. We could be made *real*.[1] We could cast off the aura of unreality that clings to these old structures of ours.

The clue to our transformation, I think, lies in a new understanding of our mission, or, rather, an understanding that, while it is by no means radically new, has been able to take into itself the unique and concrete realities of life in the nuclear age. This new understanding expresses its message in ways that can be heard by many human beings and groupings through whom God is already conducting God's mission in our darkening world.

1 Our Heritage: Conquering for Christ

Reflection upon the new always necessitates coming to grips with the old. It is not very difficult to seek out expressions of the nature of the Christian mission as we have inherited it from

2

the past. Our devotional literature, especially our hymns, is teeming with such expressions:

> Baptize the nations; far and nigh
>   The triumphs of the Cross record;
> The name of Jesus glorify,
>   Till every kindred call Him Lord.
> —*James Montgomery, 1771-1854*

> Fling out the banner! Heathen lands
>   Shall see from far the glorious sight,
> And nations, crowding to be born
>   Baptize their spirits in its light.
> —*George Washington Doane, 1799-1865*

> Lands of the East, awake!
>   Soon shall your sons be free,
> The sleep of ages break,
>   And rise to liberty.
> —*Charles Edward Oakley, 1832-1865*

> Jesus shall reign where'er the sun
>   Does his successive journeys run;
> His kingdom stretch from shore to shore
>   Till moons shall wax and wane no more.
> —*Isaac Watts, 1673-1748*

> Can we, whose souls are lighted
>   With wisdom from on high,
> Can we to men benighted
>   The Lamp of Life deny?
> Salvation! O salvation!
>   The joyful sound proclaim
> Till each remotest nation
>   Has learnt Messiah's name.
> —*Reginald Heber, 1782-1826*

> Ye armies of the living God
>   His sacramental host,
> Where hallowed footstep never trod
>   Take your appointed post.

> Though few and small and weak your bands
>   Strong in your captain's strength,
> God to the conquest of all lands;
>   All must be His at length.
> —*James Montgomery*

We note in these hymns (and in many others that could be cited) the predominance of the language of conquest and triumph. It is not accidental. Nor is it accidental that this senti-

3

ment gives way quite naturally to the military metaphor: Jesus is a captain; the Church is an army; the mission is a battle or fight; the aim of the conquest is of course to win. Everybody, everything, every nation and people should come under the sway of the one King and Lord, Jesus Christ.

Like every type of human triumphalism, this is very heady stuff! Our forebears, particularly our 19th century forebears (nearly all of the hymns quoted above stem from that era), believed themselves to be in the vanguard of a mighty spiritual crusade. The more conservative among them conceived of this crusade in terms of the victory of whatever doctrinal tradition they championed. The more liberal thought in terms of the spread of enlightened Western civilization to all the dark places of the earth. But for both liberals and conservatives it was "exciting," "thrilling," "challenging" to be involved in such a movement. The coming 20th century would be "The Christian Century!"

And for a time they seemed to have succeeded. As late as 1961, an enthusiastic Christian ecumenist could write:

> Over the past century and a half, Christianity has swept in ever wider circles across the face of the earth. No other movement in history has ever advanced so fast or so far . . . . In summary, this has been 'the epoch of largest, most varied, and most notable achievement' by the Christian religion in its two thousand years of history . . . . Christianity has become for the first time and at long last a world faith—the only candidate save communism for recognition as a universal faith.[2]

2 A Different Perspective

A little more than two decades later, this kind of observation has for most of us a hollow ring. It sounds . . . promotional! It is, besides, not very convincing. In fact it is rather embarrassing. Even if we are willing to go along with it as an historical generalization about an epoch that is past, the tone of it bothers us. For in the meantime more of us have become aware of certain things that ought to have qualified that statement (and many others like it) already when it was written.

First, we have become aware of the existence of other religious faiths and of their right to exist. Many 19th century Christians never encountered any living examples of the poor benighted heathen they sang about so lustily in church, and in relation to whom they fancied themselves endowed "with wisdom from on high." Today we have come face to face with religious pluralism—incarnated in persons with whom we live daily. You can't walk down the street of any major town on this

4

continent without encountering a whole variety of non-Christian religions—and some of the adherents may be your own children! This is a new experience for most Christians in the Western world. After the Emperor Theodosius outlawed every other religion except Christianity late in the fourth century, European Christians for centuries encountered only the Jews and, from about the 10th century, Islam. We know what European Christianity did about that! But we live, not only after the pogroms and the crusades; we live after Auschwitz. With the holocaust of the Jews, most thinking Christians have been sensitive enough to see what can happen when the Christian mission is interpreted as a militant fight *against* other religions. Even though this attempt to exterminate Israel was not conducted by organized Christianity as such, hundreds of years of blatant Christian missionary triumphalism created a climate of opinion where such a thing was historically permissible.[3] Nothing at all can *justify* Auschwitz. But out of that unspeakable evil thinking Christians have learned not only that other religious faiths *do* exist but that *they have a right to exist*—that the Christian mission is ignoble and potentially vile when it preys upon these others, "who are not of this fold."

Secondly, most people in the traditional denominations of Western Christianity have become conscious, in a way that our forebears were not, of the historically conditioned character of all religious truth. This consciousness does not necessarily lead to relativism, and it produces cynicism or atheism only in a few. What such things as historical criticism of the Bible and the critical appraisal of established creedal and doctrinal traditions have done, rather, is to introduce a little much-needed modesty into Christian truth-claims. Not only have we entertained the idea that the other religions might have some truth on their side; we have also faced the concomitant notion that there may be some falsehood on ours or at least that our version of ultimate reality is less than absolute.

This too is relatively new. It is of course a consequence of that historical consciousness that already began to seep into the Western mentality with the Renaissance: as we are creatures of time and space, all our ideas, systems of meaning, language, symbols, art, and the like reflect the particularity of our historical moment. Christianity—especially dogmatic traditions within the Christian church—resisted the implications of this modern truism longer than most other conventions of thought in the Western world. It is still being resisted, and with increasing aggressiveness, by millions of avowed Christians on this continent. But it is an insight that is hard to deny. We live our lives around consciousness, the consciousness of our historicity, even when we insist at the level of belief that we transcend history. Even the most adamant fundamentalist knows him- or herself to be living in the year 1984, the space age, the age of mass communications, the age of anxiety. It is perhaps just this knowledge, a deep self-knowledge that cannot be attributed to external pressures only, which lends to absolutist forms of Christianity that edge of aggressiveness and defensiveness that is conspicuous in so much of the new evangelicalism; for we are never so defensive as when we are struggling against our own suppressed or repressed self-awareness. The awareness of our historicity has separated most of us who remain in the mainline denominations from our own missionary traditions, however, at least in this respect: that *we no longer find it in ourselves to believe implicitly in the finality of our own belief and its articulation.* There could be a good deal of missionary zeal behind a religious faith that imagined it and it alone possessed "wisdom from on high." But if you suspect that there is a mixture of wisdom and foolishness in most human appropriation of truth, then you are not likely going to be so bold about putting forward your version of reality as if it were clearly superior. And that, I think, is what most of us do suspect at the level of basic presuppositions.

Perhaps in the process, besides, some of us have rediscovered a dimension of Reformation Protestantism that could support our new awareness of our condition as believers. I am referring to what Paul Tillich named "the Protestant Principle"—for he believed it to be not just a peripheral insight of the Reformers, but the very thing that made them "Protestants."[4] The Protestant Principle is the insistence that *God alone* is absolute, infinite, unconditioned—and therefore anything that is less than God and claims for itself our ultimate loyalty must be *protested* against. This applies not only to ecclesiastical authorities (obviously the reformers had especially Roman authority structures of their day in mind) but also to any less-than-ultimate thing that claims for itself the status of the ultimate, or has such a status claimed for it by others. It includes therefore systems of doctrine, catechisms, confessions of faith—things that the Reformers themselve produced! It includes the Bible itself. For Luther, the Bible was the most precious and indispensable witness to God's word. Our knowledge of God depends upon Scripture predominantly and finally: *sola scriptura* ('by scripture alone'). But while the Bible *bears witness to* God's Word, it is itself not to be confused with God's Word. Only Jesus, the *living* Word of God, is to be identified with ultimate Truth. And Jesus shares with every other living being this condition: that you cannot reduce Him to words, descriptions, systems, formulae, truths. Our words, even our carefully chosen words, even our creeds hallowed by time, even our Scriptures may point to God's living Word, but they can never contain it. If therefore 20th century Christians have discovered that they can no longer attribute finality to their own beliefs and theological formulations, they have only rediscovered something that was strongly present already in the Protestant Reformation, something that was lost sight of by generations of believers who, for complex historical and psychological reasons, felt it necessary to believe themselves in possession of the truth. If the insights of scholarship coming from the Renaissance have helped 20th century Christians at last to distinguish between Jesus Christ and *our historical apprehensions of* Jesus Christ, if the modern world has conditioned us to think that the language of possession is not appropriate where truth is concerned, then one must conclude that God moves in mysterious ways indeed. For what attitude could be more in keeping with the scriptural witness to the one who said, not "Here is the Truth," but "I *am* the Truth"?

Thirdly (and this may be the most important recognition of all), many of us have realized that *for Christians to go into the world today in the spirit of conquering it for Christ is to become part of the world's problem, not of its solution.* Recent and contemporary struggles on the world scene have left their mark upon our thinking at this point. For evidence of the problematic character of triumphalistic forms of Christianity we can point to the tragic situations in various parts of the world where militant types of Christianity are at the core of the strife. Sometimes this means militant Christianity against militant forms of other religions (Islam in particular). Sometimes it means one form of Christianity against another form of Christianity (Ireland). For another kind of evidence we can point to aggressive forms of Christianity on our own continent—crusades of various kinds that lend their spiritual-ideological support to equally aggressive political forces. They think that the way to deal with that other great spiritual rival for the world-soul as they conceive it (namely, Communism) is through military confrontation. In an incendiary age such as ours, when it is clear that conquering and winning and reigning are inseparable from destroying, oppressing and annihilating, a very bad taste is left in our mouths when we listen to the bellicose language of so much of what styles itself "the Christian mission" in our midst. Jesus asked, "What does it profit one to gain the whole world and lose one's soul?" We could apply this collectively to the Church and ask: What would it profit the Church to gain the whole world and lose, in the process, its soul? Is the soul of Christ's Church truly expressed in the spirit of winning, success, getting everybody onto the rolls? Is that what the mission is all about? If so, then we are truly locked into a confrontational ideology that is part of the planetary problem. Persons of good will ought to think twice before joining such a movement! But if we remain in these old established denominations of ours, most of us, it is because we do not think that mission is a synonym for confrontation.

3 What Is Our Mission, Then?

But what *is* our mission? We have gained a perspective on ourselves, on other religious traditions, and on the world itself that makes it virtually impossible for any of us to believe that our Christian mission is literally to convert the whole world to the faith of Jesus as the Christ. We are uncomfortable if not scornful when we hear other Christians talking as if that were our missionary task.[5] We do not find it in ourselves to take up the torch thrown to us by the enthusiastic missioners of our own immediate past. But at the same time we seem incapable of creating any serious alternative to that model of the Christian mission. Here and there in our midst one finds experiments. Some of them are promising, even courageous. In other quarters, Christians are obviously tempted by the success of the sectarians, or rather former sectarians (now too successful to be so named). Mostly abortive attempts are made to imitate them, to cash in on their slick electronic approach. But that style doesn't suit us. Perhaps we're too stiff, too stodgily middle-class. Or perhaps we are still authentic enough to know it just doesn't ring true.

In any case, we are confused. On the one hand we labor under the lingering impression that we should be about converting the world (and feeling gulty because we aren't); on the other hand, we hardly feel fully "converted" to anything ourselves. There is a general agreement that we ought to keep our institutions going, and therefore we continue to beat the drum for involvement, participation, good stewardship (i.e., contribution of time, talents and money to the church). But it shows up in our church giving as in other areas of our life that the "business as usual" approach to organized religion goes only so far. On the whole, it goes only as far as those classes and generations that have been reared on the sense of obligation to the chruch. And those classes and generations are dwindling, There is an unspoken— but increasingly now a *spoken* Why? beneath the surface of many congregational activities. Why should we go, work, give? Is there any compelling reason for our service, our gifts, our witness? What in any case *is* our witness? What *is* our mission?

4 The Harvest Is Plentiful

Meanwhile, things have been happening in the world—that field of our Christian witness that has so often been forgotten by the church in its preoccupation with its own problems and designs. Without rehearsing the whole flow of modern and contemporary history, we may remind ourselves of two kinds of worldly realities that are religiously significant: **The first is the growing crisis of our civilization.** It is a multifaceted crisis, combining physical and spiritual factors in a way that is almost impossible to comprehend. The physical factors, such as economic inequality and instability, the shortage of vital resources (even water), a burgeoning world population, global violence and the threat of nuclear war, environmental pollution, all are so alarming as to raise in the mind of every thinking person the question of whether humanity can survive. The spiritual factors in our planetary crisis stem in part from the impact of these dread physical realities. Social psychologists warn of the growth of a kind of programmed indifference in large segments of our populace[6]; others speak of a developing "culture of narcissism,"[7] that is, the cultivation of private happiness at the expense of public responsibility. At the same time, there is a danger that in order to stave off the various physical devastations that we face, the human community will opt for forms of authority reminiscent of Orwell's *1984* (some students of our culture think we have already done so). Humanity may survive, but might our survival be at the cost of our essential humanity?

The second (and less conspicuous) **dimension** of our present world situation that needs to enter any discussion of Christian mission today *is that precisely these critical realities have called forth from the race significant minorities that strive valiantly for the preservation of civilization against these threats.* While the majority of earth's citizens are engrossed in their own personal condition, some out of dire necessity and physical want, others because they do not have the courage of public concern, a remarkable minority sets itself against the overwhelming tide of destruction and, often at great personal sacrifice, tries to ward off the appointment with death that our civilization seems determined to keep. Organizations such as Green Peace, Amnesty International, Plowshares, Friends of the Earth and many others[8] take on the tasks of preserving disappearing species of animals and plants, or freeing the victims of political oppression and torture, or developing new sources of energy, or finding new outlets for creativity and work for those who must face unemployment in a society where one's job has too often meant one's meaning, one's very life. Books and articles appear from the desks of sociologists, journalists and others—sources from which we had come to expect pronouncements that were only blasé and often cynical—reminding us now of our human responsibility for tending the earth, and urging us to rise from our fatalized and pleasure-seeking lethargies.[9] Housewives and mothers surround the sites of missile implacements and refuse to be budged except by force. Young people march in thousands and tens of thousands in Bonn, Amsterdam, New York, Toronto, Vancouver, demonstrating against the inevitability of war, insisting that "Peace Could Break Out," and posting on their bedroom doors mottos like: "Imagine: They gave a war, and nobody came."

There is no great unanimity of purpose or motivation or program in all of these countercultural activities. In fact, though important coalitions come to be among them, there is often strife and division over the rationale and meaning, the direction and end of their various activities. But they are one in this— namely in their determination that alternatives must be found to the futureless future that is being allowed to happen on the face of this small planet. They are one in their determination that life is better than death.

Some of those who belong to this "protesting" element are motivated by explicit faith positions, whether religious or secular political creeds. But many, the great majority I suspect, are simply human beings in whom the will to life is stronger than either the pleasure principle or the "death wish." Kurt Vonnegut speaks for many of them (and to many) when he writes in the introduction of his book, Jailbird:

My father . . . was a good man in full retreat from life . . . So an air of defeat has always been a companion of mine. So I have always been enchanted by brave veterans . . . who were still eager for information of what was really going on, who were still full of ideas how victory might yet be snatched from the jaws of defeat. "If I am to go on living," I have thought, "I had better follow them."[10]

Thus against the spirit of capitulation that has stolen across the face of Western civilization, we have this motley crew of survivors urging us not to give in, insisting that it is not too late, that life is possible, that changes can be made and decisions reversed . . . even at the eleventh hour! And the disarming thing is that we find them, even the least religious of them, very often using remnants of the terminology of our own Christian past! They talk about the sacredness of life, the goodness of creation, the joy of unselfish love, The word "stewardship" is one of their favorites and they are using it in ways that jar conventional Christianity, which has so domesticated this term as to render it innocuous.[11]

5 "Go Your Way—I Send You Out "

Now let us return to our question about Christian mission, and let us ask ourselves what is surely the obvious question as we confront such a world situation: Does this situation present any scope for the imagination? Any field for deriving a new conception of our mission? Is it possible that such a context, seriously wrestled with, could inspire us with some sense of vocation and responsibility? Might we old mainline churches, languishing in self-doubt and vocational stupor, recover some sense of urgency and possibility through the prayerful and studied contemplation of our worldly context, and so be delivered from our spiritual dullness and our business-as-usual mentality? Do we perceive here anything like a field that is ripe for harvest?

As we consider such questions, we should at the same time remind ourselves of *two biblical assumptions concerning the mission of God's people: The first* is that *it is not, to begin with, our mission, but God's.* The testimony of the New Testament is that in Jesus as the Christ, God has entered into the sphere of human history in a decisive way to redeem it. Eternity has invaded time. The world has been visited. Its transformation is being undertaken now through the Spirit, that Spirit whose character and aim have already been disclosed in the suffering love of the Cross. God is at work healing the creation, making of the tragic kingdoms of earth a kingdom of peace. This is not a project of the church, not even of the "Church invisible," let alone any of the visible entities called churches.[12] The Church is not the kingdom, and the kingdom is not the Church's enterprise. The Church is that community (for the New Testament a relativity small community—little flocks here and there) that is privileged to glimpse, now and then, the work that *God* is doing in the world, to bear witness to it, to articulate its meaning, to participate in It and help it to happen.

And the *second* biblical assumption we should bear in mind as we try to decipher what is going on around us today has to do with *the character of this work of God*, this kingdom-building. What is its inner aim, its *telos*?[13] Is it to get as many people as possible to say that they believe in Jesus as their Lord and Saviour? Not according to the parable of Matthew 25:31 ff., which expresses a concept by no means unique in the Bible: namely, the idea that the self-conscious kind of religious conviction that is all too often identified as true faith may be a stumbling-block to genuine obedience; that there is no necessary connection between the right words and the right behavior. Is the aim of God's mission then the creation of a great ecclesiastical institution—one church of the one world? Are we to envisage the global dominion of Jesus, if not through the old-fashioned conquest based on the power of armies then through the use of economic superiority, the power of evangelistic technique, or even the power of ideas? No, apparently not. Typical of most scriptural reference that could be offered in this connection, the sending out of the seventy contains an implicit criticism of power tactics of every sort. Those who are sent out are to take with them . . . nothing! They are to travel light, without even a change of clothes. No mention is made of pistols! They are to be defenseless in a violent society, vulnerable to strangers, dependent upon the generosity of those to whom they are sent. They have only their words. Their only power is the power of the message itself, and it is not *their* message. Moreover, its power has nothing to do with their powerful (or perhaps ineffectual) articulation of it. The message has power only because there are, in the world, in the very towns and villages to which the seventy are to go, persons who have already been moved by God's pervasive Spirit, who are in some real sense already participants in the kingdom. The children of peace (let us call them) are already there. They will recognize the messengers of peace, receive them, commune with them, work with them. What the seventy discover (to their astonishment!) is not how effective they are, how glorious their own untapped human potential, communication skills, etc. What they discover is that God was there before them. God's mission precedes ours—our mission is only follow-through. We shall only confuse God's work if we imagine that to the subtle and usually un-self-conscious effects of the divine Spirit upon the lives of our worldly sisters and brothers it is now our duty to superimpose thick layers of doctrine and religious formality. The work of God in which we are permitted to participate is not about creating ideological armies any more than it is about creating armies of the sort that they got up in the Middle Ages to fight "the infidel." The kingdom-building of God is not about aggression of any kind, whether the conquering of bodies or the conquering of souls—"thought control," as Orwell called it. *God's* kingdom is the antithesis of all oppression, domination, manipulation. Its essence is contained in that word *shalom* that has worked its way back into our Christian speech once more. Peace! Yes, but "not as the world giveth." Not just the absence of hostilities, but a condition of well-being, justice, mutuality of concern, harmony between all creatures, gratitude for being. God's kingdom means that quite apart from our witness to it, God is already "at work in the world to make and to keep human life human."[14] That is the goal of God's mission: the nurture and enhancement of life.

6 The Kingdom of God Has Come Near To You

So again we ask ourselves: Does it begin to appear what our mission might be? Does such reflection upon the mysterious working of the divine Spirit in history give us any new perspective on present world events? In a world where thousands die daily because of greed and violence, while others, fearing death, court it by retreating from public life and pursuing their private pleasures and pains—in such a world does it strike us what it might mean to be participants in a mission whose aim is abundance of *life*? In a society where there are already, as we have noted, uncounted thousands of ardent "children of peace" at work, waiting to receive all who come in the name of the kingdom of peace, does it occur to us what might be entailed in the mission of the Prince of Peace?

Let us be very serious: We find ourselves living at a moment in the history of Earth when the struggle between the forces of life and death, light and darkness, *shalom* and annihilation is perhaps more transparent than ever before in time. Existence on this planet, maybe the existence *of* this planet, is in grave question. Moreover, we have just reminded ourselves, insofar as we believe ourselves to be disciples of Jesus Christ in such an historical moment, we are persons who are by definition called to be on the side of life and against death. Can there be, therefore, any question about what our mission is under such circumstances? Surely Christian mission today means the stewardship of life in this kingdom of death. If we could start from that premise, then we would have unburdened ourselves of a great weight of lethargy, guilt and self-preoccupation. The despondency that now so often clings to our discourse on mission, unfulfilled mission, would be exchanged for a new sense of being needed. For what greater mission could any human society have in a world like ours than the stewarding of life? And the tired, predictable, and slogan-ridden appeals for good stewardship could also then be dispensed with; for stewardship, on such a premise, would no longer be a nagging thing on the periphery of our church life, but a way of designating the very core of our faith. In a time given over to the courting of death, the gospel: stewarding life!

Thus the kingdom has indeed come very near to us. Perhaps it has never been so near. In less decisive, more ambiguous times, it has been difficult even for astute persons of faith to

13

discern the presence of God's kingdom. Very often God's kingdom was mixed up, in the mind of the Church, with the aspirations of seemingly progressive societies; so that, as we notice earlier, generations of 19th century Christians could set out for the dark places of earth assuming that in taking with them the accoutrements of Western civilization they were the bearers of the heavenly kingdom. It is still possible, of course, to live under this sort of delusion. Yet the distinction between God's kingdom and the kingdoms of this world, with their weapons set to destroy each other and their ways of life programmed to rape the creation, has become so palpable in our time as to be almost inescapable to ordinary common sense. Ours is in short something like the situation described by Luke in the sending of the seventy: a clear differentiation exists between the kingdom we are called to announce and the ways of the nations. It is the difference between day and night, between life and death.

7 The "Religious" Rejection of God's Kingdom

The kingdom of God has indeed come very near to us in our time. But there is another theme in these Scriptures. It accompanies the good news of the kingdom of God like an antiphon. It is found in the Lukan passage cited above; it is found everywhere in the Bible. God offers God's kingdom of Shalom; it is like a great banquet feast of life . . . *and people are always declining the invitation*!

We should not delude ourselves: the people who say no to God's kingdom are not just "those others," the people who stay away from church, the people to whom *we* go only to be rejected. By itself, the Lukan passage might suggest such a thing, as if there were no rejection on the part of the seventy themselves. But from the rest of these Scriptures we know that the seventy also turned away. In fact most of the meaning of the Lukan passage is lost unless it is remembered that not only the seventy but eventually also the central core of the disciples community—the twelve—all "forsook him and fled." There is a no to the kingdom of God running through the whole history of the Christian church like a leitmotiv. It is not surprising that it can also be heard among us today, as we contemplate our position in a world to which God's kingdom has come very near.

Nor is it accidental that the rejection of the kingdom, as this theme is presented in the Scriptures of both Testaments, is strongest on the part of the most religious elements in the society. The greatest critics of Jesus, like the greatest critics of the prophets of Israel before Jesus, were those reputed to be the

14

most scrupulous in their devotion to the Deity. In the name of their religion, i.e., in the name of their established systems of belief, ritual and morality, they rejected the invitation to open their lives to the wider, uncharted regions of the world to which God's unconditioned love willed to manifest itself. It was not new, this behavior, in the case of Jesus. All the prophets and lawgivers of Israel experienced the same thing. All the reformers and saints of the church have experienced it too. It is almost a law of the history of belief: prophetic faith is rejected by none so adamantly as by "the religious"; because "religion," more often than not, is the name that we give to that type of ritual conservativism that has found in certain definite dogmas and rules of behavior a kind of shelter from the unknown, the mysterious, the anxious-making dimensions of life. And prophetic faith is (quite rightly) perceived by this mentality as an exhortation to leave the safety of dogmatic sanctuaries, and to follow the Spirit of God into the wilderness, into the marketplace, into wide open spaces where there is no security and much temptation! Religion cannot simply ignore prophetic faith, not at least in the Hebraic-Christian tradition, because in spite of itself religion within this tradition must carry with it a high respect for the faith of the prophets. So the religious ones who honor the prophets (and build tombs for them, said Jesus) are deeply challenged by prophetic utterance, and very often, in consequence, deal with it severely!

It is not surprising therefore that contemporary resistance to God's kingdom as perceived by prophetic faith comes most vehemently from the side of "true believing" Christian conservativism. For this avowedly most religious expression of the Christian religion discerns in the prophetic challenge to the church to open itself to the pain of the world a threat to its own security. This security is based upon systems of thought and rules of life that are satisfactory only so long as the pain and complexity of worldly life are kept out. That is why, with the conspicuous augmentation of worldly crises of every kind, the most consistent and most vulnerable forms of Christian "true belief" today have had to construct *whole alternative environments*, "Christian" environments, so that their adherents will not have to be exposed too directly to the real world.[15]

To such forms of Christian community, the suggestion that the Church's mission is to follow a God who will lead precisely into the very heart of this world's darkness is a grave threat. The threat does not lie in the judgment that the world is indeed a dark place; Christian conservativism has always maintained that! The threat lies, rather, in the suggestion that following our God into that dark place means entering into sympathetic identification with those whom we find there, sharing the burden of their

15

existence, and only discovering *in company with them* what it might mean to have light for this darkness. The whole raison d'etre of "religion" in this sense of the term is that it insulates its devotees from all that darkness, sin and anxiety of worldly life; and to propose, as prophetic faith always has proposed and still does, that the community of belief is a body called to suffer with Christ *in* the world—this is to attack the very foundations of religion. Religion is glad to consider itself a beacon to those who are drowning in the seas of life. But it resists fervently the prospect that in order to save the perishing it may have to risk its own life.

In other words, the mission as conceived by religious "true belief" is to offer the world the spiritual security of whatever code of belief has been identified as "true," "orthodox," by this or that sect. "Evangelism" refers to the promulgation of the accepted creeds and codes; its object is to extract from as many people as possible the profession of belief along these lines, complete, usually, with the standard phraseology, bodily gestures, modes of prayer and address, tastes in music and entertainment, etc., that stand as symbolic tokens of belonging to that particular grouping of the faithful. A less definitive, less doctrinally- and symbolically-codified expression of belief (such as the one I am proposing here), a sense of mission that involves solidarity with the suffering of the world and the risk of losing one's religious security blanket—this is entirely unacceptable to "true believers." They resist any participation in any kingdom that is not quite explicit about its rationale, and not able to pronounce the right formulae. In short, the stylized profession of belief has become for them the end of the mission.

I cannot read the Bible without concluding that this kind of mentality is a gross distortion of the end to which Jesus points—and the prophets before him. It is an ideological mentality,[16] in content but not in form distinct from any other ideological posture, including that of doctrinaire Marxism against which this type of Christianity so often positions itself. Ideology is the dark, temptation side of theology. Theology points to mysteries that it knows it cannot define; ideology is what happens when theology succumbs to the (very human) desire for finality of understanding, and takes refuge in dogma against the mysteries of God and life. In saying this, I do not intend to make light of belief and of its articulation in doctrine. Our beliefs constitute for us the very driving force that sends us out into the harvest, which keeps us from seeking our own pleasure and security and gives us courage to risk life in a world that is probably inhospitable. Our beliefs and our frail attempts to express them in coherent ideas and systems (theology) are the means to the end of our mission.

16

But they are not as such the end! The end of our mission is not the profession of the faith, whether this means our own profession or the profession of those to whom we believe ourselves sent. Profession of the faith may be the means, or part of the means; but the end is not *profession* but *confession*—a very different thing in fact. One may understand much, believe much, proclaim much of what the Church professes and still not confess the Christ. For confession requires that one has sensed the point where the gospel of the kingdom is being most seriously attacked and undermined, and has found somehow the courage to confront the attacker in life, word and deed. How often in the history of the church has it happened that the profession of the faith has served as an excuse for faith's confession? By the same token, the Scriptures know well of the possibility that the faith may sometimes be confessed by those who do not know the Name. "Many whom God has," said St. Augustine, "the church does not have; and many whom the church has God does not have!" As I read it, those people and groups in the Bible who make the profession and preservation of their own doctrines and rituals into ends are regularly chastized. They are the ones who pass by on the other side, allowing death to take its course. The whole notion that the Christian mission consists of a great and prolonged drive to baptize, confirm, marry and bury everybody always has been questionable on biblical grounds. But today this mentality is not only scripturally questionable, it contributes to the general betrayal of the gospel of life. For it can only lead to aggressive and oppressive behavior; and in a world plagued to death by "little orthodoxies" that "vie for our souls" (Orwell) nobody needs a Christianity that constitutes one more predator on human life.

8 Mission Does Not Mean Expansion

Resistance to the identification of Christian mission with the stewardship of life comes, however, not only from ideological forms of the Christian religion; it comes also from a more subtle spirit, a spirit present within all of us, the spirit of pride. After 20-odd centuries, most of which permitted the Christian religion a place of great prominence in the scheme of things, it is hard for Christians and Christian communities to assume a less glorious stance. We are conscious of ourselves as heirs of what in our church history texts and our general ecclesial rhetoric is regularly called a noble heritage, a thrilling story, and the like. We have seen that 20th century Christians are conscious in a particular way of a segment of Christian history (the 19th century) that saw a phenomenal expansion of the Christian religion through the world. We have in fact been conditioned to think of Christian mission in terms of Christian expansion. Study the missionary documents, maps, and surveys provided by any respectable history of the church. Those periods during which the church was growing in numbers and in terms of worldly power and influence are invariably described as the periods of great *missionary* endeavor. The equation, mission equals expansion, is so firmly entrenched in our thinking that numerical gains in church statistics invariably are interpreted in terms of missionary success, whereas periods of waning membership, financial loss, and the like, are automatically assumed to be times during which the Christian mission was failing. By such logic, Jesus' own mission must be regarded as a failure, for even the few who followed him proved in the long run faithless and fell away. But perhaps the logic of the cross must call in question the whole assumption that faithfulness to the mission means the expansion of the missionary community.

Still, we are powerfully committed to the assumption that missionary success will express itself in quantitative terms; and the most immediate implication of this is that we are loath to assume for ourselves the role of a minority. It's a comedown, what I have been suggesting here. It's asking a church that moved through centuries "like a mighty army" to become a community of servants. *Stewards, not soldiers!* It's suggesting that we let ourselves be dispersed, risk being lost in the great welter of the global struggle for life, risk not being able always to identify ourselves and blow our various doctrinal horns, risk our lives, risk the reputations of our ancient ecclesiastical foundations themselves, for the sake of an endangered planet and its mortal inhabitants. It's suggesting that we put the reign of peace before our concern for right belief and form; that we associate with people who may be operating out of questionable motives and beliefs that are perhaps antithetical to our own; that we make ourselves vulnerable to misunderstanding, rejection, suffering . . .

But might that not be nearer to the logic of the cross than the assumption that faithfulness to the mission inaugurated by the crucified One would be rewarded by tangible success of the sort that could be fed to computers?

9 Thy Kingdom Come . . . On Earth

In any case it is foolish for us to continue giving our credence to that assumption. If mission means expansion then we are indeed in a state of radical disobedience, because the kind of evidence that *can* be fed to computers indicates that these old classical forms of the church are on the wane.[17] It is possible that we could become extinct in a couple of hundred years. I am not suggesting anything especially dramatic: certainly we should go out with a whimper, not a bang. In all probability we shall continue in the world for quite a while even without significant changes—refuges for the nostalgic, shrines for certain classes of people, now more and now less competitive with other little orthodoxies.

But meanwhile the God of life will have gone elsewhere to look for laborers in the harvest, because our God is not interested in preserving antiquaries or sustaining museums of religion. God is for *life*, and God will find apostles of life outside the sanctuary if the sanctuary becomes a mortuary.

But why should we settle for such a future? Why should we allow ourselves to be driven out of our old wineskins by the fear that they will burst? New wine is being offered us. A new lease on life is being held out. The end of Christian mission as Christian expansionism could be the beginning of Christian mission as a real participation in God's kingdom-building.

What I mean is this: The thing into which God is trying to lead us in these last decades of "The Christian Century" is no paltry undertaking. Certainly it is shorn of the *kind* of glory Christendom has habitually coveted, the kind that Jesus, being tempted, turned down! In the kingdom God is building in the midst of death's kingdom, systematic theology will not be queen, and the church will not be a great property-holding multinational, and Christian armies will not go off to glorious death, and churches will not count their significance by counting up their membership rolls and seeing how many very important people are in that number. All that, along with mission as expansion, will exist for the church of the future only as the record of a bad temptation, rejected by Jesus and picked up by his Church, which finally achieved little if anything of true significance thereby. But there is another kind of glory (for the most part untried by empirical Christianity) that can become, at the end of the Constantinian Era, a real alternative. The New Testament is already full of metaphors depicting this alternative model of the Church and its mission: salt, yeast, light, a mustard seed, a little flock. In short, the Church could become a worldwide fellowship of significant minorities—*koinonia* that, without great fanfare, would help to give birth to the life that God is creating in the midst of death's kingdom.

And so as not to end this meditation in a burst of generalities and pious rhetoric, let me quickly indicate some of the things that I mean by that last sentence:

First, in the titanic struggle for life that is occurring in contemporary history, Christians can (if they will) add important dimensions of depth and color to visions that are often, without their kind of witness, flat indeed. Life *is* more than bread! Bread is certainly not insignificant for our tradition of Jerusalem. In these matters of the body we can join hands with others, like the Marxists, who refuse to "spiritualize" human life and consequently call in question every ideology that through neglect of the material dimension of human existence legitimates structures and authorities that leave the poor in their poverty and the rich unjudged. Life *is* bread. But it is not bread *alone*. Therefore it belongs to the Christian mission, not only to work with whoever strives for justice and material equality among peoples but also to keep alive that spirit that reaches out for the wine of the soul, for meaning, for joy. We should not forget, when we think of Christian mission today, the experience of the Christians in Czechoslovakia before 1968, how, in their dialogue with the Marxists, it was the Marxists, finally, who begged the Christians: "Tell us what you mean by transcendence! We need to hear from you what *end* you have in mind, what goal human beings ought to seek after they have been fed! Do not let us forget the wine in our struggle to obtain bread!"

Second, in the search for fullness of life in a planetary community that transcends national and regional loyalties, Christians can bring to bear an ecumenical (catholic) sense of the world which, for want precisely of this, our world is torn between imperial striving that may end in Armageddon. There is a touching paragraph in Jonathan Schell's *The Fate of the Earth:*

> ... governments, still acting within a system of independent nation-states, and formally representing no one but the people of their separate, sovereign nations, are driven to try to defend merely national interests with means of destruction that threaten not only international but intergenerational and planetary doom. In our present-day world, in the councils where the decisions are made there is no one to speak for man and for the earth, although both are threatened with annihilation.[18]

There is no one to speak for humanity and the earth! If Christians cannot hear in these words an invitation to the kingdom of God and its enterprise for life, then we have lost all imagination and are beyond help.

Third, in the struggle for life against death, Christians are able to bring from the treasures of their tradition and faith a vigilance for others—especially for minorities, for the victims, for the enemies of the dominant forces in any civilization. There has never been an empire that did not crush some and favor others. Christians worship a God before whom all are equal, and who, so far as God favors any, favors those who *lack* favor in their worldly setting. Vigilance for the victims of any culture is the essence of the stewardship of life. Victims represent the principle of rejection, alienation and death present in every form of community, and unless they are heard and their cause championed, that destructive principle will eventually consume the whole society. It would be well to keep this in mind today as we listen to the cries of the poor, the unemployed, the native peoples, women, and other segments of our society who are giving voice to forms of injustice and alienation that are no longer on the edges of our society but are symptomatic of a universal malaise.

Fourth, in the struggle for life against death, Christians can keep alive a vision of the *end* for which this struggle is undertaken and towards which it could move. "The churches," wrote Paul Tillich, "always should be communities of expectation and preparation. They should point to the nature of historical time and the aim towards which history runs."[19] The symbol of the kingdom of God represents not only the possibility of life that is always being inserted into the process of time, but a vision of the ultimate goal of being that encourages and at the same time prophetically judges every existing embodiment of life. The kingdom *of God* gives human kingdoms a basis in something more life-affirming than the human will as such, which is always partly life-negating. At the same time God's kingdom provides a critical norm on the basis of which human kingdoms may be interpreted, judged and changed.

In these and many other ways, the Christian mission into which we are being beckoned today contains, if we are open to it, every bit as much by way of challenge as could have been felt by our 19th century forebears. In a real sense it should be even more challenging for us because, while their concern was the expansion of Christendom, the thing that calls for our ingenuity and faithfulness is the survival of the creation itself. And let us not fret over the prospect that we shall have no opportunity explicitly to proclaim the gospel and evangelize the nations! If we are true to the call to be stewards of life in the kingdom of death, we shall certainly never lack for opportunities to tell our contemporaries ... the reason why. But the converse is also true: If we are *not* faithful to the mission that is life's stewardship, then by itself all our proclaiming and evangelizing will come to nothing.

DIALOGUE

Question: At the end of the Gospel according to St. Matthew, Jesus says: "All authority in heaven and on earth has been given to me. Go therefore and make disciples of all nations, baptizing them in the name of the Father and of the Son and of the Holy Spirit, teaching them to observe all that I have commanded you . . . ." (28:18b ff.)

Does this not mean it *is* the church's task to try to convert everyone to a conscious belief in Christ?

Response: It is hard for us to read a passage like this—the so-called Great Commission—without assuming that is indeed what Jesus meant. For we read this statement with the eyes of believers who have inherited some 16 centuries of Christian expansionism. Thus we take to the reading of this and similar biblical statements a great many unexamined assumptions—for instance the assumption that the only people who could ever be described as disciples of the Way would be persons who had been duly indoctrinated in the Faith, baptized believers.

Yet in the newer Testament itself there are many indications that Jesus himself understood discipleship differently. The mere acknowledgment of belief seems not to be what counts in his view, but *being faithful* in deed and in life. Remember the parable of the two sons when one said yes to his father's bidding and then didn't do it, the other said no but then went out and did the work he'd been asked to do (Matt. 21:28 ff.)? Moreover, Jesus seems well aware of the fact that there are many who actually are doing the will of God who do not act out of a specific sense of obedience to God's will (See, e.g., Luke 9:49–50).

Clearly the newer Testament here and in many other places assumes that as Christians we do have a mission. And this mission certainly has to do with bringing about changes in the world and in the hearts of human beings—*repentance*! But is it after all so clear from our scriptural sources that the goal of our mission is to bring everyone to an explicit belief in Jesus as the Christ? The Great Commission as it stands suggests to us that making disciples necessarily involves baptizing people in the name of the holy Trinity. But New Testament scholars have been telling us for decades that the "trinitarian formula" in this very passage probably indicates that it is an "interpolation" (something added later, after the church had devised its trinitarian theology of God). Besides, our own long history ought to have informed us that baptism as such could hardly be regarded as the goal of our mission. The vast majority of "Christians" throughout history seem to have come to baptism quite automatically, regarding it as a formality. The test of discipleship is whether it entails an ongoing change of direction (metanoia) in one's way of being in the world, not whether one is able to recite dogmas and produce baptismal certificates. "By their fruits you shall know them."

In saying this I by no means intend to belittle the importance of an explicit faith in the Christ. But we are reducing the gospel to ideology when we make the articulation of belief the end of the matter. All the sacraments, the preaching, the theology and symbolism of the church are there to enable us to be disciples in the world, not as ends in themselves.

Question: In your meditation, and in your response just now to the first question, you used the term "ideology." I don't understand this term, I guess. I thought all thinking was "ideological."

Response: Of course from one standpoint everything that we think about, write about, speak about emanates from an "ideology." That is, every idea, whether we realize it or not, reflects or presupposes a whole understanding of the world—of reality. So in one way or another we are all "ideologs," and the basic question is therefore whether we *know* that about ourselves.

In other words, there is in all of us a natural tendency to formulate concepts, mental constructs, about the world, life, the totality. This is a necessary process. We could not live without it. We could not communicate without it. We could not have community without it. It belongs to our nature as thinking beings—"rational animals," as Aristotle said.

For example (to bring the discussion down to more concrete terms) I have in my mind certain pre-understandings of my wife and children. Over the years with them I have formed impressions about their identity, who they are, what they like, how they are likely to respond to a given situation, etc. So when I meet them each morning at breakfast I do not meet them as perfect strangers but as familiar persons, images of them that I carry about in my mind.

But this very *necessary* process is also fraught with danger. The danger is that the images that I have of my wife and children will become "graven images": that is, that I will allow them to be hardened into fixed concepts—ideas so thoroughly crystallized that the real persons who are my wife and children will have difficulty breaking through the concepts I have created of them. How many families are destroyed by this very process!

It is the same with our conceptualizing of the totality, the whole of reality. We can give so much loyalty to our own intellectual-spiritual pre-understanding of the world that the world as it actually *is* has a hard time getting through to us. In fact, we use our *ideas* about the world to shield ourselves from the real world.

This is not just a danger, however, it is also a great temptation. For the real world is very hard for us to live with on a day-to-day basis. We would like the world to stand still, but of course it never does. So it is tempting for us to resort to ideas, systems of thought, political theories, religious dogmas, etc. in which it does seem to stand still. We create in our heads the sort of world that God didn't create for us, a world that stands still, that has (like Holiday Inns) "no surprises," that does not forever challenge us to rethink it.

And the worst part is: sometimes some of us become powerful enough in our system-making to cause the world, or large parts of it, actually to *conform* to our images of it!

Question: You seem to have a very low opinion of religion! Is religion always a bad thing in your view?

Response: There are of course many ways of using the term "religion." Historians and sociologists can with perfect right speak about the religions of the world and about Christianity as one of them. But in theology we have to make distinctions when we use this term, because if we pay close attention to the Scriptures of both testaments we do find there a consistent criticism of the religious impulse—even a polemic against it. Karl Barth, perhaps the greatest Protestant theologian of the modern era, wrote, "The message of the Bible is that God hates religion."[20]

What Barth means by this is that the God described in the continuity of the Testaments hates that impulse within us human beings that tries to get hold of God and control God— as Jesus put it, the attempt to "take heaven by storm." Religion in this sense is what is being described in the myth of the Tower of Babel (Genesis 11): quite understandably, people want security; so in the anxious quest for this elusive commodity they build a city and a tower into the heavens. They want to achieve sufficient proximity to the Deity to exercise power over the Deity and thus control what transpires on earth.

Because of this biblical polemic against the spirit of religion, many theologians in our time have distinguished between

"religion" and "faith." If the Tower of Babel illustrates the religious impulse, faith is illustrated by the story of Pentecost. In religion, the human quest reaches up to try to influence God—and in the process reaps alienation within the human community (they couldn't understand each other at Babel). Faith on the other hand is our response to God's reaching down (grace), and its consequence is the overcoming of alienation between human beings (at Pentecost they all understood one another, though they spoke different languages).
I would not write off religion simply as a bad thing. It is there, so to speak. I mean, it's a *human* thing, part of every human community, even when some people try to pretend otherwise (as do Marxists). But we should be careful to distinguish between this natural human impulse of fallen humanity and Christian faith. In the church, and in each one of us, religion and faith are found side by side, in various mixtures. But it is still necessary to distinguish between them.

Question: Throughout your address just now, you seem to assume that the Christian churches are losing ground, are "on the wane," as you put it once. But is this really so? In my town, there are more people in church today than there were a decade ago, and the President of the United States says we've found our faith again as a people.

Response: When I say that the old, established forms of the church are on the wane, I am not thinking only in quantitative terms. In a way, the quantities are not nearly so significant as the qualitative aspects of our status as churches. By qualitative I mean things like how earnestly we take our belief, whether it influences our everyday lives deeply, and so on.
But even quantitatively we are experiencing losses, and have been for a long time. This may not be noticeable in the local scene, but it is true of the so-called First World and Second World generally. According to one of the most exhaustive studies produced within the last few years, *The World Christian Encyclopedia: A Comparative Study of Churches and Religion in the Modern World, A.D. 1900–2000*[21]:

"Christianity has experienced massive losses in the Western and Communist worlds over the last 60 years. In the Soviet Union, Christians have fallen from 83.6% in 1900 to 36.1% today. In Europe and North America, net defections from Christianity—converts to other religions or to irreligion—are now running at 1,820,500 former Christians a year. This loss is much higher if we consider only church members: 2,224,800 a year (6,000 a day). It is even higher if we are speaking of only church attenders: every year, some 2,765,100 church attenders in Europe and North America cease to be practicing Christians within the 12 month period, an average loss of 7,600 every day.

The *Encyclopedia,* which was produced under Christian auspices, goes on to note that in the Third World (especially Africa and South and East Asia) the numbers of Christians are on the increase, and that this increase mitigates somewhat the losses in the First and Second Worlds. It also, of course, tends to shift Christianity towards the Third World, a shift that will probably become more conspicuous in the decades ahead.

Such statistics do not, of course, indicate very much about the *quality* of the church today. How many of those who remain in our Western churches are seriously *practicing* Christians, *thinking* Christians? For how many is Christianity more than merely a civil religion? The most active and growing forms of the church, especially in North America, are the fundamentalist and spiritualistic sects: What does this do to the quality of the Christian faith?

There is a tendency on this continent—particularly in the United States, and more particularly still in affluent suburbia and the South of the U.S.A.— to project onto the world picture the apparently lively character of Christian belief in one's locality, or on one's TV screen. In many places in the U.S.A. one can get the impression that Christianity is surging upwards. This is not even true in the United States, though it is a convenient promotional myth for those who think that numerical success is what it's all about.

Question: I was interested in what you said about the need to be concerned for the victims of any society. Do you mean that they are like a weathervane? That what happens to them tells us something about the whole society? And if that is so, what would you say about the return to the death-sentence in many communities here?

Response: You understood my point very well. History again and again demonstrates that the way in which a society treats the poor, the weak, the mentally-handicapped, its indigenous peoples, minorities of other races, women, children, the sick, the dying and the dead (in other words the persons who are not in a position to measure up to the standards of the strong)— that this tells one more than anything else about the internal weaknesses of that society.

It seems to me very obvious why this is so. The fact is that *all* human beings, being finite and sinful, are *vulnerable.* Eventually every one of us becomes something of a victim, if not on account of our race or sex, then perhaps on account of illness; if not because we are poor materially, then perhaps because we are poor spiritually or intellectually; if not because we are tempted to crime, then because we may grow bitter, or find ourselves alone, deserted by those on whom we expended our love; and eventually we all shall die. The more a society bases its "values" on the virtues of youth and vigor and success and strength, the more it victimizes, finally, not just a few people on the fringes, but everyone. It seems to me that our affluent societies of the North have come very close to this situation.

The specific illustration you use is very instructive in this connection. If the only way in which a society can deal with persons who give way to the violent impulse is to kill them, this society is making a very telling statement about itself. It has been demonstrated many times over that the death-penalty does not deter most murderers, since most of these crimes are crimes of passion, committed by close relatives or friends. It is a sign of our deep but repressed frustration about the violence that is present *in our whole society* that our only response to the persons who are driven to the extremes of this same logic of violence should be: Kill them!

Question: At the end of your presentation you said that if we are really stewards of life in the kingdom of death we'll have plenty of opportunities to tell the reason why. I found that provocative, but I need to know more about what you mean by it. Will you be returning to this theme later?

Response: Yes, to some extent. I also developed that idea in my book, *The Steward*, particularly in the chapter called, "On Being Stewards." It seems to me that in a world like ours, where there are so many reasons for despair, and where in consequence so many good and gifted people opt out of the world and cultivate their own private lives, it's a pretty unusual thing to discover men and women who really dedicate themselves to the world's well-being. I think you know what I mean: You meet the same people again and again at the meetings, the marches, the work among the underprivileged, the fund drives, everywhere. Even in a big city like Montreal I am always running into the same people at such events and in such places. Not all of them are Christians, of course—not by a long shot! But all of them make you wonder: What are they in it for? What's in it for them? What drives them to do this? Why don't they stay home like most of their neighbors and enjoy the hockey game or paint the back fence?

Nothing arouses people's existential curiosity so much today as do other people who go out of their way to assume public responsibility—usually at the cost of personal sacrifice, and often risking their lives. Persons like Mother Teresa and Helder Camara and Jean Vanier are great curiosities of our Age. Cynicism, when it is kind (and much pop psychology too), writes them off as altruists—people who get their kicks out of doing good deeds. But we know there's more to it than that. So we are driven to ask them: Why? Or when they *do* explain themselves, there is a sufficient degree of preliminary interest in those who have heard of their lives and deeds that they are listened to.

Christian witness that is offered in response to such curiosity makes a difference. Little difference is made by sheer verbal witnessing, no matter how noisy it is! Most of it is strictly gratuitous.

SECOND MEDITATION

THE CONTEXT OF OUR MISSION: A COVENANT WITH DEATH

. . . hear the word of the Lord, you scoffers,
who rule this people in Jerusalem!
Because you have said, "We have made a covenant with
death,
and with Sheol we have an agreement;
when the overwhelming scourge passes through
it will not come to us;
for we have made lies our refuge,
and in falsehood we have taken shelter";
therefore thus says the Lord God,
"Behold, I am laying in Zion for a foundation
a stone, a tested stone,
a precious cornerstone, of a sure foundation . . .
And I will make justice the line,
and righteousness the plummet;
and hail will sweep away the refuge of lies,
and waters will overwhelm the shelter."
Then your covenant with death will be annulled,
and your agreement with Sheol will not stand;
when the overwhelming scourge passes through
you will be beaten down by it.
As often as it passes through it will take you;
for morning by morning it will pass through,
by day and by night;
and it will be sheer terror to understand the message.
For the bed is too short to stretch oneself on it,
and the covering too narrow to wrap oneself in it.
For the Lord will rise up as on Mount Perazim,
he will be wroth as in the valley of Gibeon;
to do his deed—strange is his deed!
and to work his work—alien is his work!
Now therefore do not scoff,
lest your bonds be made strong;
for I have heard a decree of destruction
from the Lord God of hosts upon the whole land.

Isaiah 28:14–22

1 Bargaining with Death

The ancient author of these words could not have dreamt of bombs that would destroy the whole planet. He could not even have conceived of a planet in our sense—that small green-blue sphere floating in a great sea of infinity, the planet Earth. But he knew rather well the human habit of pursuing death as a way of resolving the seemingly irresolvable problems of life. What better way to describe the situation of the nations of earth in the last quarter of the 20th century than to say that they have made a covenant with death? There has been a tacit agreement among the powers that be that life, if it is to endure, can only be guaranteed by a dangerous pact with death. Each of the two great empires of the planet has given almost total credence to this pragmatic credo, while the other nations alternate between envy and fear, protest and complicity. With the kind of fervor usually reserved for fanatic forms of religion, the empires pile up the weapons of megadeath. According to some statisticians, the U.S.A. has enough bombs to destroy every major city in its own land 55 times over, while the U.S.S.R. has only enough to destroy every U.S. city 40 times each. But this is disputed by many leading citizens in the West and so becomes the occasion for evening the score, surpassing "the enemy," and so on it goes . . . and where it stops everybody knows!

The particulars of this historic scenario are of course entirely contemporary; but the concept behind it is very ancient: You placate the gods of death and destruction in order to guarantee for a little longer what you are calling "life." The flaw in this religion is also ancient: when you give so much credence to death your whole life is conditioned by the worship of death, and so the life you thought to preserve becomes tainted with the smell of the mausoleum even before the funeral. "The Arms Race Kills: Even Without War."[1] And in more ways than one.

There is indeed no area of our life today that is free from the cloying odor of death. Recently a young Roman Catholic parish priest told me that he had asked the members of his Westchester County youth group whether they expected that a nuclear holocaust would occur in their lifetimes. One-hundred percent of them answered: Yes. Not even in the young, vigorous, affluent places of our culture is it possible to keep the smell of death out of one's nostrils. Many of the most beautiful and sensitive among our young seem bent upon self-destruction. I refer not only to the high suicide rates among the young, but also to the *almost*-suicidal pursuit of oblivion in drugs, alcohol, in sexual abandonment, and in forms of tribalism that seek to drown the consciousness of self. Lewis Thomas, in his provocative essay, *Late Night Thoughts on Listening to Mahler's*

THE CONTEXT OF OUR MISSION: A COVENANT WITH DEATH

Ninth Symphony, makes what I think is the right connection between such youthful behavior and the reckless posturing of nations:

> The man on television, Sunday midday, middle-aged and solid, nice-looking chap, all the facts at his fingertips, more dependable looking than most high-school principals, is talking about civilian defense, his responsibility in Washington. It can make an enormous difference, he is saying. Instead of the outright death of 80 million American citizens in 20 minutes, he said, we can, by careful planning and practice, get that number down to only 40 million, maybe even 20. The thing to do, he says, is to evacuate the cities quickly and have everyone get under shelter in the countryside. That way we can recover, and meanwhile we will have retaliated, incinerating all of Soviet society, he says. What about radioactive fallout? he is asked. Well, he says. Anyway, he says, if the Russians know they can only destroy 40 million of us instead of 80 million, this will deter them. Of course, he adds, they have the capacity to kill all 220 million of us if they were to try real hard, but they know we can do the same to them. If the figure is only 40 million this will deter them, not worth the trouble, not worth the risk. Eighty million would be another matter, we should guard ourselves against losing that many all at once, he says.
>
> If I were 16 or 17 years old and had to listen to that, or read things like that, I would want to give up listening and reading. I would begin thinking up new kinds of sounds, different from any music heard before, and I would be twisting and turning to rid myself of human language.[2]

That the young should be most deeply affected by the prospect of a civilizational holocaust is of course not surprising; nor is it a new phenomenon. Such behavior in the young has perhaps been in the air ever since the fruits of the Industrial Revolution began to cause the sensitive to doubt that humanity has a purpose. Thomas Hardy in *Jude the Obscure*, written in 1896, poignantly described this phenomenon—the effect of societal anxiety upon the young. Father Time, the pathetic name given to a boy of 12 who seems incapable of joy, murders his two little siblings and then hangs himself; and Jude, their father, reports that . . .

> ". . . the doctor says there are such boys springing up amongst us—boys of a sort unknown in the last generation—the outcome of new views of life. They seem to see all its terrors before they are old enough to have staying power to resist them. He says it is the beginning of the coming universal wish not to live. . . ."[3]

One of Hardy's contemporaries, Sigmund Freud, named this phenomenon "the death wish" (*Todestrieb* = a drive towards death). What Freud may not have realized, what perhaps Nietzsche understood better, is that such a drive, which may be as old as Adam (certainly it is as old as Hamlet), is deeply enhanced in societies that pay so much respect to death, societies that have made a covenant with death. For when the will to life is no longer sustained by external social structures, goals and attitudes, then the tender, internal psychic thread that binds us to life is strained accordingly; and in the young that thread has not had sufficient time to prove itself, to strenghten itself through all the myriad relationships and experiences that under normal circumstances fasten us firmly to our existence.

Yet it is not only the young who are sacrificed to this Molloch. The old, too, in our society suffer from the presence and preoccupation with death by which all the structures of our world are conditioned. What does it mean, I wonder, to come to the end of one's life, even if it has been a relatively satisfying life, facing the prospect that the little treasures of the spirit that one may have to pass on are not wanted? This is the first time in history when, at their dying, human beings have had to contend existentially with the thought that their microcosmic end may coincide with a cosmic omega, the demise of the macrocosm. This raises the question of *meaning* in its most bitter form. I could accept my dying, somehow, when I felt that something good lived after me, something to which I might even have contributed a little. But with the prospect of civilizational decay or destruction, the death of individuals seems all the more pointless.

And then, in between youth and old age: the parenting, the working, the tending and caring and saving, *all of it oriented towards the future*. But the society that has made a covenant with death has to reckon with a futureless future. How many of the lives all around us—within us—are spoiled by this morbid knowledge? It is not, of course, only the presence of the bomb; it is a whole host of things out of the dreadful modern Pandora's box, things far more concrete and more scientifically describable than anything envisaged by the ancients who conceived the mythic imagery of Pandora's box. The bomb is only the most potent symbolic and real of these concretizations of death. It is the point where our bargaining with death becomes most transparent and most crass.

2 The Death of the Spirit

There is however something even worse about our covenant with death than its known and felt consequences. It is the largely uncharted, truly mysterious deadness of spirit that is induced at the subconscious level as a way of coping with our conscious awareness of more than our human spirits can cope with. It is as if the bomb had already fallen, a sort of super neutron bomb that killed human spirits while leaving human bodies more or less intact.

Robert Lifton of Yale, basing his conclusions on studies of the victims of Hiroshima and other phenomena, has named this our "psychic numbing."[4] The human psyche is not capable of taking in threats so all-encompassing as the multidimensional end by which our age is dogged. So in that act of self-preservation that the psychologists have named "repression," we create a kind of spiritual indifference to whole segments of reality that constitute our daily experience. We condition ourselves not to hear certain items of news, not to be moved by reports of mass slaughter or starvation in this or that remote part of our globe (what does remote mean on Spaceship Earth?). We hear with the hearing of the ears names such as Lebanon, Grenada, Afghanistan, El Salvador; but the messages encoded in these names are not allowed to reach our souls. We assume a *quantitative* stance toward reality, as it were—the sort of comprehension of data that is no longer able to assign *moral* significance to the data. Some of us, to be sure, are able to recite impressively many of the negative facts of our environment: that two-thirds of humanity is undernourished; that acid rain is killing off the Black Forest and ruining the ancient treasures of Europe as well as half of our own continent. That whole species of animals and plants are disappearing from earth forever at a rate of something like a species a minute. Such quantities no longer evoke a qualitative response from millions of us. Thus we move on from day to day, victims of something akin to Isaiah's "overwhelming scourge," but living on two levels of consciousness: on the one we plant and plan, sow and reap, save and spend, work and sleep as if the familiar process were going to continue ad infinitum; on the other, deeper but largely unacknowledged level of knowing we are aware that all of our activities are begging the question of the end, both in the sense of their goal (telos), and in the sense of their cessation.

The uncanny thing about the process of psychic numbing, however, is that it cannot be confined to the more shocking data of our collective and private lives; it becomes a very way of being in the world. The repression of some aspects of experience is, to be sure, necessary to life. As Ernest Becker put it, repression is to human beings what instinct is to animals.[5] We are not made in such a way that we could stand being exposed to "naked anxiety" (Tillich). That is why in the Christian story it is only the Christ who suffers the total abandonment of the cross. But when persons and whole societies trespass the thin line between *necessary* repression and the use of the repressive instinct as a way of life, we can expect that our lives will be affected not only at the public level but in the most intimate corners of our being and our relationships. Thus for many of us living in the society that has made its covenant with death, depth of feeling at any level is hard to achieve. Many of our citizens manifest an incapacity for feeling. Genuine communion with other human beings, really listening to one's acquaintances and colleagues, feeling moved by their stories is rare among us, and people from other, older or more primitive societies are astonished by our superficiality. Half the conversations one overhears at parties or in public places sound like replays of television commercials or soap operas. Love is reduced to its glandular sensations. Marriage lacks the dimension of compassion, so that when the passion goes there is nothing left to sustain it. Children are wanted by fewer and fewer couples in the modern West, in the Second World as well as the First. The reason is not obscure: Children cry out for feeling, for warmth, for involvement in life. They elicit from us what so many of us do not want to give, feel that we cannot give, perhaps. To love a child is to open up the whole wound that we are so diligently attempting to close, the wound of anxiety that is inflicted upon all who care, who are committed to life.

I know that this is hard talk. It conjures up the specter of doom and gloom, and seems to fall into that sphere of pessimism that we, good citizens of the Brave New World, do not find compatible with the image of cheerfulness and well-being that we like to project (even when we are feeling anything but cheerful and well). The one sin that is left in our middle-class circles, including the ecclesiastical gathering-places of our class, is negativity. Perhaps we Protestants, especially those of us who hearken back to the Reformed tradition, are ashamed of the gloomy aspects of our own past, of Calvin and Knox and Edwards with their long and mournful countenances, their talk of total depravity, their angry sermons. I certainly do not propose that we return to all that. But I do suggest, and earnestly, that we Christians must let go of our liberal moorings and our bourgeois cheerfulness sufficiently to allow ourselves to be led along the contemporary Via Dolorosa. If we cannot stand in "the environs of Golgotha" (Barth) then neither shall we be able to bear witness to the One who assumed for us all of the cross that is at the center of that bleak scene. We are not called to die on that cross; but we are called to stand in its proximity. If Christians cannot endure taking into their consciousness the terrors that our secular neighbors spend so much time and energy repressing; if we, with our living symbol of life emerging at the point of death, of healing breaking through where only disease had been before, of shalom as the unwarranted but real outcome of human violence, if with the cross and resurrection of our Lord at the core of our faith we Christians cannot waken our minds to the darkness at noon, then how can we expect people who possess no such cornerstone, no such foundation for reflection and meaning in ife, to open themselves to such realities. The whole point of the cross at the center is to give us the courage to be truthful about what is wrong with the world; for there is no evil, sin, or death to which our God is stranger. God is there in the midst of it. We may open our eyes to whatever scourges threaten us.

We must open our eyes! Because only the truth can save us. Let us not deceive ourselves. The way of an exaggerated repression, of psychic numbing, is *part* of the way of death, the most poisonous part. Nothing will be changed, everything will be permitted, death will encounter no opposition whatsoever if all earth's citizens, particularly those of the First and Second Worlds, indulge the need to hide the truth and play a little longer the game of happiness. "A society based on the pursuit of happiness," said the great German scientist and lay-theologian C. F. von Weizsäcker, "cannot survive; only a society based on truth can survive." To be a Christian, if it means anything at all, means to have—no, to be given—the courage of truthfulness. "The theology of the cross," said Martin Luther, "does not have to call evil good and good evil; it can call the thing what it really is."[6]

How can we "respectable" Christians, so unused to prophetic utterance ourselves, though we read the prophets in our churches with all due solemnity—how can we learn to call the thing what it really is? To call a spade a spade! Our polite categories for naming the world are the categories of a tired Liberalism. They are simply inadequate! Our world has become sick unto death. Kierkegaard saw it coming more than 100 years ago. And the sickness cannot be attributed to some foreign agency in which we have no part. Certainly it cannot be confined to militant Communism, as so many of our First World citizens want to believe; or to Western Europe, which some of our leaders seem to feel could if necessary be sacrificed in the game with death. Since we are calling for truth, we must at last realize that many of earth's billions today are convinced that the source of the world's sickness lies in the heart of this favored continent of ours, this place that outwardly can still seem so full of the promises of life. Not only in the Third World, but in Western Europe as well, multitudes of highly intelligent and sincere human beings, not a few of them our fellow-Christians, have concluded that North America is more to be feared than any other quarter of the globe. It has come to seem to them that most vulnerable channel through which Sheol could one day spew its lava over the face of the green planet. For the most part this judgment does not stem from any ill-will. It is very often voiced by persons who love this New World of ours and the energy, vitality, and inventiveness for which it is world-famous. But they find us a vulnerable people all the same and for one basic reason: we combine two incendiary ingredients, great power, technical power, and great naivety, the naivety that is born of the determination always to think positively . . . especially about the infinite potentiality of our own power.

We rush to our defense. They are wrong! They do not know us! They have not grasped the depth of our undying love of life. Well, it may be so. Or have they perhaps realized all too well our love for our *way* of life, our dogged insistence that we shall go on living this way come hell or high water; our determination to preserve intact our hard-won freedom, protect our standard of living, our gross national products, our happiness, regardless of what that determination might mean for the rest of the human race and for the inarticulate creation? Listen! The pact with death of which the prophet speaks is not made by the losers of history but by those who have so much to lose. They will go very far in their bargaining with oblivion: "Better dead than Red!" They will bank upon power, horrendous, untapped and untested power, even when they have every indication required by human intelligence to know that the power in which they trust is ultimately *self*-destructive. It was this same prophetic recognition of the unthinking defensiveness of those who *have* that caused a British political analyst in 1962, in the wake of the Cuban missile crisis, to write:

> It is at least possible, as things stand today, that the hand which formally and technically releases large-scale nuclear war on the world will be Christian.[7]

3 The Religion of Death Behind the Politics of Death

But this leads to the final observation that must be made about the society that has covenanted with death. It is that for Isaiah, as for the whole prophetic tradition in one way or another, the society that bargains with death is invariably a religious one. The prophet who has given us the metaphor of the covenant with death is not railing out against godless unbelievers but against fervent believers. "True believers!" In the name of God they are ready to consign their world to nothingness if that is the only way they can preserve their own souls, their own properties and values, their prosperity. "Oh, the scourge shall not come near to us," they insist: "We have made a convenant with *Mot*!" Mot is the Phoenician god of wheat, of fertility, and (naturally) of the underworld. Mot! It just happens that the name of this god of power and success stands in juicy homiletical proximity to the Hebrew word for death: *Moth*! The prophet is a poet and he cannot resist this provocative etymological tidbit: in the name of the god of fecundity and prosperity, the leading people of his land have in fact been worshipping death. "We have made a covenant with Mot," they boast; but the prophet knows that this apparent security is the ultimate insecurity. The demonic gods of those who seek their own salvation in a suffering world always demand as their due the souls of their worshippers. "Those who seek to save their lives shall lose them," said Jesus in the line of this same prophetic wisdom.

The gods of the underworld and of death are not always known as Mot, or Ba'al, or Molloch. Might they not also be called (under certain circumstances) "the Lord," "the Spirit," "Jesus"? One thing we can be sure of, if we follow the biblical story closely, is that the politics of death are always undergirded by the religion of death, and there is no name so sacred to death that it is above being used for demonic purposes. If a "Christian" hand does press the fatal button, that hand will have been guided by a mind and sanctioned by a spirit steeped in the language of Christian, apocalyptic righteousness. For millions of the citizens of this continent, Christianity *means* a faith in which "the fate of the earth" has already been sealed. Already planet Earth has been consigned to oblivion. It is already *The Late, Great Planet Earth.* The book by that title, the best-selling book bar none of its decade (it sold more than 15 million copies), only carries to its simplest conclusion the longstanding Christian ambiguity about this world. This world has been so consistently denigrated and bemoaned in most of the classical traditions of our religion that an objective reading of Christian history must often cause unbiased readers to conclude that with few exceptions Christians could only entertain the idea of *salvation* in company with the idea of world *destruction*, if not damnation. Even in many of our most profound expressions of faith, even (let us be honest) in some biblical expressions lifted out of the total context of the Scriptures, the process of redemption seems to presuppose the demolition of the created order. Hal Lindsey is unfortunately not unique. He is in some ways a contemporary amanuensis of the long line of world-despising apocalypticism, simplified for the TV generation and invested with an aura of "the scientific" on account of the convenient contemporary potential for world-smashing introduced by nuclear warfare.

In one of the sequels to *The Late Great Planet Earth* (for it seems that the end of the planet does not send one to one's closet to pray or one's rooftop to wait nowadays, but to one's typewriter to dash off more best-sellers). Lindsey writes:

Think of it! During this generation, at any moment, Jesus Christ might come back. We might find ourselves with just the average mundane day—suddenly, the next moment we're face to face with the Lord! We realize that our bodies are different—that we have been transformed into new bodies which will never know sorrow, or sickness, or aging again. We'll look over and see loved ones who have died long ago. There will be a reunion in the sky along with Jesus Christ.

What a way to live—with the constant excitement that today—TODAY—may be the one which will signal that it's all over but the shouting in His presence!
Keep your hope at an exciting pitch, because the time is really here. He's coming SOON! Live it up to the hilt for Jesus . . .
We're in the homestretch. Let it all out and drive to the finish where Jesus is waiting![8]
He is talking about the end of the planet Earth. He is talking about nuclear holocaust. And he's excited! It's "The Rapture" . . . for a few. For the many, including "much cattle" (Jonah 4:11), it is just the bitter end.

4 For Want of a Vision

Thus religion, "the Christian Religion," for so it calls itself, adds to the secular and political covenant with death its cultic dimension, its sanction. And the pronouncements that we have been hearing from very high places in our society indicate that this religious sanctioning of the reckless bargaining with death is entirely effective.[9] It creates at the popular level a sense of abandon born of the belief that, since God is on our side, we may go very far in our bargaining with death. One even discerns a kind of eagerness for the great show-down just beneath the surface of our existing in this society. Aftr all, the technological society does not expend all that energy, ingenuity and money on the machinery of destruction without feeling the urge to try it out. And when this is combined with a spiritual form of security that ensures us in advance that nothing *ultimately* destructive could happen to us if we did try it out—"the overwhelming scourge will not come near to us!"—then what is to prevent us from the most extravagant boasts in the face of our alleged enemies? Thus the mood of our society, where it is not a bored, narcissistic cynicism about public life and meaning, is far too often an adolescent exhilaration at the prospect of Armageddon. Like macho young males behind the wheels of their souped-up cars, we are some of us ready to flirt with death, feeling ourselves indestructible, or perhaps drawn by a deep fascination with death, a sort of social necrophilia.
How, in the face of this complex pact with death, can those

of us who find ourselves in what we are still trying to call "the mainstream of Christianity" present an alternative vision? The trouble is, I think, we are lacking precisely that—a vision! Visions, prophetic, compelling visions, are born in the night. Like the prophet Daniel: "And in the night I saw visions . . . " To see visions you have to have experienced the night, and in our old, positive-thinking, liberal Protestant churches we are unaccustomed to the night. We sense that it is getting dark, but we hesitate on the edge of the night and scurry about for our pocket flashlights—our little insights, our ethical positives, our imperatives. Stewardship is one of them. We tell each other that we should be stewards of God's creation. No doubt! But it is still at the level of should for most of us, that is, at the level of law. We have not made the transition to gospel, that is to a vision of reality that can move us and our hearers from the posture of moral necessity to the realm of real possibility. No one, not even those of us who are moved by the rhetoric and the symbol of stewardship, is really going to respond to this imperative unless we are able to demonstrate far more convincingly than we have that this exhortation to be stewards is founded on a viable, profound and compelling vision of reality itself.

And so the question to which we have to address ourselves most assiduously is this: Can we enucleate a *gospel* in which the whole work of God, culminating in the Christ and forwarded by the Holy Spirit, is a *world-affirming and life-affirming message*? If we cannot do this, or if we continue to waffle and to manifest the age-old Christian ambiguity about the fate of the earth, then there will be no use announcing the law of Christian stewardship and beating the drum for a more responsible public attitude towards the world. It makes sense to care for this creation and to take responsibility for all its creatures; it makes sense to look for people and time and money to enable a church to engage in the promulgation of worldly stewardship—all of this makes sense *only* if our fundamental vision, our gospel, depicts this world unambiguously as the object of divine redemption, transformation, and shalom.

Today the religion of death and the politics of death that it sanctions are wonderfully powerful, more powerful, probably, than at any time in human history. Listening to the average news broadcast, even the hardened secularist is tempted to think in Armageddon terms. Not only do we now possess the machinery to put into effect humankind's age-old hatred and revenge against the earth and its Creator; but today we seem also to be at the weakest point in the human search for historical meaning and the courage to believe in the human project. The spirit of Homo sapiens, late 20th century style, appears to lack the imagination and the courage to believe, all by itself, in anything. Only a faith that can show itself strongly on the side of life can expect to give chase to the religion whose basis is a covenant with death.

Is Christianity such a religion? Is the mission in which we are all involved *in fact* the enhancement of life, the healing of creation, the incarnating of justice and of the love of God in the on-going process of world history? Millions of our fellow-citizens on this continent have claimed the Christian faith as cultic backing for the culture that has shown itself ready to covenant with death. Can we reclaim Christianity for *life*? Is our gospel, with its central symbol reminding us of the reality of human suffering and death, nevertheless and fundamentally a toast to life? *L'Chaim*?[10]

DIALOGUE

Question: I admit the truth of much that you say about our society—the behavior of our young people, the way we treat the old, even the fact that we turn off our minds so much. But isn't it after all a one-sided picture? There are still happy young people and satisfied older people; and at least the truth is there for us to get hold of, it isn't hidden from us as in some societies.

Response: I certainly agree with you that there are happy young people. I have the privilege of living intimately with four of them. There are older people, too, who know that they are much better off than might have been the case in earlier societies. In my country, for example, they can count on a very enlightened concept of government-sponsored medical care. I also concur with your statement that much truth is available for the asking. In a way, there is so much of it that we don't know what to do with it—the information explosion, it is called. At the same time, we shouldn't wax too eloquent about that. Much is kept from us, too, or manipulated by the media.

But as for your main point, the one-sidedness of what I have said in this meditation, I think I shall dispute that, or at least interpret it. Christian faith and theology have always manifested a particular concern for what is wrong with the world. This is our heritage from prophetic biblical faith. As one of the Latin American theologians of liberation has stated it in contemporary language, all responsible thought today begins with the recognition that the world is not the way it should be.

The "should be" is very important in that sentence. Christians are people who have some feeling for what should be: there should be justice, there should be peace, there should be love between persons, there should be freedom . . .etc. So they are particularly sensitive to the lack of these things, not on their own account, but on account of those who suffer most from this lack: the victims. (See the first *Dialogue*.)

If you consider the prophets of the older Testament, and if you think about Jesus' ministry in the line of these prophets, you will remember that the most characteristic note struck by them all is that something is wrong. The most common object of their scorn are the people who are going about and saying that everything is fine: the "false prophets" who cry "Peace, peace" where there is no peace (see Jeremiah 6:14, 8:11, etc.). Prophetic faith is especially conscious of what is wrong with the world *because it has a strong sense of what could be right.* It speaks out of a vision of the possible.

There is another reason why, in our particular context, Christians have to be outspoken about what is wrong. This is because of the fact (yes, it is simply part of our whole make-up in North America) that we are so prone as a people to believe in our own basic goodness and innocency. The villains of the world are always somewhere out there. If things are going wrong with us then, like normally healthy individuals who suddenly get sick, we begin to accuse someone of poisoning us: it's the communists or somebody. The truth of the matter is that we on this continent are the center of one of the great empires of our time. Our (relative) economic prosperity is purchased at the expense of many other of the world's peoples. Many economists insist that the much-lauded recovery in the U.S.A. today is a direct result of military spending. Our nuclear arsenal threatens the whole globe, and all the more so because our neurotic need to believe that "I'm all right" makes us more than a little trigger-happy in relation to our alleged enemy.

Nothing is going to be done about the world situation by people who won't consider what's wrong with it.

The real greatness of North American society (to me, this is particularly true of the United States) is its capacity for self-criticism. I sense that this capacity, which was so effective during the war in Southeast Asia, is in a weakened state today. Too many people want and need to think that our house is in order.

There are many things to be grateful for in North America. But self-deception is not one of them.

Question: About the high suicide-rate among our young people: Isn't this due to things like unemployment, drugs, alcohol, pornography, family break-up, sexual uncertainty, all that sort of thing?

Response: Yes. But you have to go deeper and ask, Why? Why are young people so unnerved by the prospect of no job? Why do they take to drugs, drink, crazy sex and all the rest? Why do they want to have their minds blown, their heads turned on (i.e. turned off)? Such things as you have listed are only secondary causes at best; more accurately described, they're consequences, symptoms. In a society that is basically healthy (life-oriented, to use the language I have been employing in these meditations), the natural tendencies towards self-doubt, vocational and sexual uncertainty, escapism and so on—things that somehow belong to the period of adolescence and youth—are offset, largely, by social patterns and structures and rituals that undergird the positive life-urge in the young and help them through such critical stages. But if the society itself is suffering from future shock, a crisis of confidence, or what-have-you, then the support it normally can give to its own younger or more vulnerable members is missing, and instead its messages to them are highly ambiguous or covertly destructive. I think this is doubly so in societies that, like our own, seem incapable of honestly facing their crises. Such societies tend to give off exaggeratedly *positive* messages at the rhetorical level while in their deeds and in unspoken ways they tell their young, "We're lost."

Question: I had a hard time swallowing your negative approach to TV religion—Hal Lindsey and all that. We have something in this country called freedom of religion. I don't think we should be so critical of what other people believe. Belief is a matter of personal choice. Who am I to say that what somebody else chooses to believe in is wrong?

Response: I'm all for religious freedom, but let's not fool ourselves: Religion is a public matter and not just a private one. When you have whole great blocks of the American public today openly supporting a political party, you can't just relegate religion to the closet. Religion (and in this case we're talking about the Christian religion, at least according to its own opinion) is being used today to back up questionable policies in the areas of peace and war, international relations, economics, race and sex issues, etc. I would recommend that you read in this connection an article by Jim Wallis in *Sojourners* called "The President's Pulpit." Wallis claims that "On at least five occasions in the last four years, President Ronald Reagan has referred to his belief that Armageddon (the final battle between the forces of good and evil at the end of the world) may be fast approaching"; Wallis attributes this to the kind of support the President is getting from the "Christian Right," with its apocalyptic approach to belief. When you put together the military spending of the present American administration and a religion that assures its adherents that "the End" will usher in "the Rapture," you have a dangerous combination of ideas.

We liberal-minded Christians of the old, established denominations like to think that all religion (like our own?) is basically good (innocuous?). Better some religion than none. Better wild religion than atheism! So we think. But we should think again, especially in the light of the biblical criticism of religion (see the *Dialogue* following the *First Meditation*). In this year of 1984, when we are celebrating the Barmen Declaration[11] of the small confessing church under Hitler, we would do well to remember that Herr Hitler would probably have had a hard time getting anywhere politically if it had not been for right wing German nationalistic religion on the one hand and liberal let-it-be-ism on the other.

I'm not saying we should attack individual Christians, certainly not the Mrs. Smiths and Mr. Joneses who send their five-dollar donations to some TV evangelist. But we must try to engage these religious movements themselves, and try to get at the causes of them. They have become very powerful on this continent, defining for ever greater numbers of people the very *essence* of Christianity. I, for one, am not prepared to have the Christian faith co-opted by the spirit of apolcalyptic, world-rejecting religion. Its popularity is directly related to the widespread public desire to escape the harsh realities of this late-20th century world. What is needed is not a religion that caters to this desire, but a faith that changes those realities.

Question: Would you please say a little more about what you mean by necessary repression? When does repression become a dangerous thing?

Response: If every morning before I got up I lay in bed and reminded myself consciously of all the dreadful things out of my past and the frightening things that might occur in my future, I suspect I would never get up out of bed. I would be psychically, and probably physically, debilitated. You have to keep the lid on quite a lot of your life, just in order to get on with the business of living. Martin Luther in his Augustinian monastery at Erfurt, before he discovered that he was "justified by grace," was so tied up inside himself with guilt and despair that he couldn't even pray, let alone do theology or help his fellow monks.

But there's an invisible line between healthy repression and repression that is sick. If in order to get myself into gear for my working day I not only push down into the subconscious abyss some nasty little thoughts that want to present themselves to my mind, but must also brush aside or ignore my wife and children, my colleagues and students, and anyone or anything that will remind me of the real world in which I am living, then there is probably something wrong. To put it in a sentence: repression becomes pathological when it ceases to be engaged in the service of living and becomes an insulating psychic blanket against the world in which I am called to live.

Question: It's all very well to talk about having a vision, but so many of the visionaries one encounters are just woolly-headed idealists. Totally unrealistic! Who doesn't want peace, for instance? But how can you have a peaceable kingdom when there are other people in the world you can't trust?

Response: Or perhaps when you can't even trust yourself . . . ? Well, I will be addressing this question later on, but for the moment just this: You say the visionaries you meet are unrealistic. I'd say that most of the self-announced realists I meet are just fatalists underneath their so-called realism. Basically what they are assuming is that this is the way it is, will be, and must be. I don't even call that realism; because if you follow history very closely you see that new and unpredictable, unprecendented things are always in fact occurring. Just because something has been that way often, or is reputed to have been that way, it does not follow that it must be that way, or even, for that matter, that it will.

But aside from that, I wonder how content Christians can be with the kind of realism that pits itself against visions. I agree that Christians are called to be entirely honest about what they find in the world, especially (as I have already said) about what's wrong with it. But aren't they also called to believe in the providence and love of God? If the answer is yes, then they have to entertain visions of what the world might look like if God really did love it and providentially care for it.

THIRD MEDITATION

THE BASIS OF OUR MISSION: GOD'S COVENANT WITH LIFE

And in that day, says the Lord, you will call me, 'My husband,' and no longer will you call me, 'My Ba'al.' For I will remove the names of the Ba'als from her mouth, and they shall be mentioned by name no more. And I will make for you a covenant on that day with the beasts of the field, the birds of the air, and the creeping things of the ground; and I will abolish the bow, the sword, and war from the land; and I will make you lie down in safety. And I will betroth you to me for ever; I will betroth you to me in righteousness and in justice, in steadfast love, and in mercy. I will betroth you to me in faithfulness; and you shall know the Lord.

> *And in that day, says the Lord,*
>   *I will answer the heavens,*
>   *and they shall answer the earth;*
> *and the earth shall answer the grain,*
>   *the wine, and the oil,*
> *and they shall answer Jezreel;*
> *and I will sow him for myself in the land.*
> *And I will have pity on Not pitied,*
> *and I will say to Not my people,*
>   *'You are my people';*
> *and he shall say, 'Thou art my God.' "*

—Hosea 2:16–23

1 For Love of the World

Can we reclaim Christianity for Life? This world's life?

At its core, the newer Testament answers that we not only can do this but we must—unless we are to mock the whole rationale of the incarnation and humiliation of God's own Word, for . . .

"... God so loved the world that he gave his only Son, that

46

whosoever believes in him should not perish but have eternal life.

For God sent the Son into the world, not to condemn the world, but that the world might be saved through him." John 3:16, 17

We live in a world that, once again, has made a covenant with death. But we live here as witnesses to a God who has made a covenant with life. The new covenant in the life blood of Jesus is God's ratification and renewal of God's ancient, creational Amen to life; it is the final seal on the divine determination to mend the creation.

Christians who have discerned the signs of our times know that their gospel, therefore, stands in direct confrontation with the dominating spirit of our age, that spirit emanating from the bargaining with death about which we thought in the previous meditation. The mask of life, which death-serving empires heretofore have sometimes worn with deceptive grace, has in our time been pulled off. No matter how they paint and prop up our leaders in today's empires, it is hard to disguise the grim reaper they have all, poor souls, been bargaining with. Underneath the bid for empire, very close to the surface of public life, so that even the innocent are suspicious, the grin of megadeath shows forth. Death's grin, like that of Lewis Carroll's Cheshire Cat, does not belong to anyone in particular. It transcends our leaders, who one after another fall into line with what they perceive as a necessity. (It is uncanny how almost without exception the political, military and scientific leaders of our society, as soon as they near retirement or actually leave office, caution the world against the very policies that, in the heyday of their power and influence, they themselves pursued. While in office, they seem drawn by forces over which they have no personal control.) In the post-Hitlerian world, it is no longer possible to locate the culprit—though, pathetically, we still indulge in that sort of child's play. Death speaks through many voices: big business, big labor, management, bureaucracy, government, the press, organized crime, the military. . . . But when you try to pinpoint it and run it to earth you feel like Don Quixote chasing windmills. The elusive smile fades, leaving only a poor, wretched human being without much wisdom and even less courage, or offices full of people who are just doing their duty. Technology (as some name death[1]) "is leaderless" (Martin Buber).

Yet Christians know that to say yes to life today must mean saying no to those leaderless forces that are driving our civilization to the brink of the abyss. Hard, and perhaps impossible, as it is to identify the abode of Moth, of Ba'al, we are bound as those being incorporated into the Body of the one who came that the world might have life to seek out and root out the works of death.

In short, we are participants in a struggle, stewards of a political gospel, political in the most rudimentary sense: namely that as inheritors of God's world-saving love we are pushed over to the side of the preservers of earth and against the forces of destruction. Our gospel is political in the sense that it has at its heart the life of the *polis*,[2] and therefore we cannot be indifferent about the destiny of what St. Augustine called the human city (the city of Man). Just because we are citizens of God's *polis* (the city of God), the earthly city is all the more real, all the more meaningful to us. For in Jesus Christ "the kingdoms of this world *have become* the kingdom of our God." There is no heavenly kingdom that is ontologically separable from the fate of the earth. If we continue to use the distinction between heaven and earth at all (and perhaps we should not), then let us use it for theoretical purposes, not as if it were absolute. Heaven is not some *alternative* to earth, allowing us to sit lightly to earth's fate. Heaven, eternal life, is a way of speaking about the quality of life that God intends for the earth. No, it is not *confined to* earth; for God's love encompasses the universe, visible and invisible; it is not containable in finite creation, it is infinite. But this same love is applicable in a very concrete sense, and with all its intensity and its mystery, to earth. Even that reputedly most unearthly of the New Testament's writings, the Apocalypse of St. John, makes the renewing of earth the object of the divine judging-love. There is no Lindsey-like rejoicing over the apocalyptic judgment that the prophetic traditions of the Bible believe must be visited upon this world. Yes, judgment there must be! But the judgment is for the cleansing of the world, not its demolition. " . . . and I will say to Not my people, 'You are my people'; and he shall say, 'Thou art my God.' " Hosea 2:23

2 "Whither Thou Wouldst Not"

The realization that we have been grasped by a grace that thrusts us into the political arena comes as a surprise to many Christians today, even as a shock! Particularly in our liberal democratic societies, Christians have taken for granted in the past that the Christian faith, whatever its language and its forms, is basically in line with the highest values and noblest goals of society. We Christians have been able to think of ourselves as supercitizens of these nations and commonwealths. Our religious convictions could seem to have the salutary effect of adding sincerity and depth to the fundamental precepts of our culture at large. The separation of church and state, where it has pertained, has allowed us to distinguish between religious and civil dimensions of our world view; but we have been able to assume on the whole that it is a unified view of the world, that at least in its ethical expression the religious dimension would normally correspond positively to the general public morality and the goals of the state.

But today, to the enormous surprise of many of us who are involved in both church and society, this suddenly has changed. The secular media's coverage of the recent meetings of the World Council of Churches in Vancouver is one kind of documentation of this change. Even the World Council, which is not notoriously political, turns out in the public eye to be tainted red and "humanistic" (apparently a very bad thing to be), while of course to the more conservative elements within church and society its activities are seen as positively subversive. All of this, chiefly, because the World Council has made certain signs, during the past decade, of being on the side of justice, of helping the poor and oppressed, of being in favor of life instead of death.

This disturbs many people in our churches. I suspect we are all a little nervous about this new reputation we are acquiring for being lovers of the world. We are ordinary people after all. We do not want to be perceived as unworthy citizens, social misfits, or rebels against the dominant stream. For the most part, we are good, middle-class Americans, Canadians, West Germans, or what have you. We are hardly your average radicals. But suddenly it seems as if our belonging to the church is (to use our Lord's terminology in his cryptic address to Peter at the end of John's Gospel) 'carrying us whither we would not go.' In spite of ourselves, we find that we have to stand out against governments, against technological and economic structures, against trends and policies and values that are deeply embedded in our way of life. This way of life of ours is showing up more and more conspicuouly as a way of death; and as persons who are more or less serious about our faith we find ourselves carried by that seriousness along paths of thought and action that frequently surprise ourselves as much as they surprise our associates and friends. This is not something that we planned. Most of us are not critics by nature. It is just a kind of inevitability that takes hold of us the more the gap widens between our culture's pursuit of what it seems to want and the gospel that we have heard and are hearing. The masks have been removed from so many of the principalities and powers that determine our collective life. We find we are no longer able simply to assume that our God is working through the state, the governing authorities, the dominant classes and forces of our First World nations. Perhaps there is divinity behind these structures, but perhaps it is the divinity of the Ba'al or of Mot. We on this continent have always been prone to regard ourselves as another Israel, a new Israel in a new land of promise. But " . . . what if we are a Babylon rather than an Israel?" asks President Donald Shriver of Union Theological Seminary: "And even if we are (like Israel, what if we are) an Israel on the verge of exile rather than an Israel triumphant in Conquest? It is one thing to identify with an ancient 'chosen people.' It is another to decide which time of their history speaks most truly to one's own."[3]

The experience of discovering the inevitable political dimension of the gospel came to some of us in a unique way in June of 1983. We had met in Erfurt, East Germany, in the very cloister where Martin Luther before us had begun to find out that the Christian message can drag one kicking and screaming into the political area. There were 30 of us from eight different countries, and representing in our small number each of the three worlds—First, Second and Third—into which economic and political issues have divided our one world. We had come to Erfurt during that year of Luther celebrations to discuss a very complex theological theme: "Reformation Theology for Today: Luther's Justification Theology and Calvin's Theology of Covenant in Relation to the Quest for a Just Peace." It sounds innocent enough, doesn't it? Many of us who had come to Erfurt from the West were prepared, I think, to tackle the week-long project in the rather typical, serious but detached way of historical and systematic theology, for we were most of us professional theologians. You remind yourself of the traditions; then you apply them as best you can to the present situation. Fine!

But we were not prepared psychically for what happened to us there. Suddenly, having to discuss such a question in such an environment made us realize something about the change that has come over church and world in our time, and more particularly over the relation between church and world. Let me elaborate:

In East Germany there are two peace movements. Well, there are two in the West, too, of course, only with us the distinctions are blurred. In the German Democratic Republic and other east bloc countries, the official peace movement (the only legal one) doesn't try to mask its assumption that peace is based on sheer power: one keeps the peace by having so many bombs and other weapons of warfare that the other side wouldn't dare. So the government in East Germany comes right out and announces what the peace effort means for all loyal citizens: "Frieden schaffen—gegen NATO waffen!" (Work for Peace—against NATO weapons!) The unofficial peace movement, comprised mostly of confessed Christians and humanists, gives no credence to the religion of deterrence—the covenant with death. Its motto is: "Frieden schaffen—*ohne* waffen!" (Work for Peace—Without Weapons!) It is strictly outlawed. To be seen wearing the badge of this movement (the famous plowshares badge), or even a white patch where the badge used to be, is to invite arrest. I always think the East German Christians are fortunate in one sense: everything is so much clearer there!

In this clearer atmosphere, then, it became more apparent to us First World Christians too that the quest for real peace, as distinct from the quest for military dominance and imperial clout, sets one apart as a Christian from the dominant streams of one's society. In that context we found out in a new way that our Christian affirmation of *life* put us into an immediate struggle with powers on both sides of the tragic curtain. Only as we realized our common opposition to the processes of death at work in both of our worlds, and how these processes have deadly effects particularly on the Third World (from which some of our members also came), only then did we open ourselves anew to the gospel of the cross to which Luther bore such timeless witness. That gospel does not skirt around the reality of death but goes precisely to the heart of worldly darkness, descends if necessary into hell itself, and begins from there, with the crucified Christ, to find the way back to life.

With this by way of background, then, let me quote a few sentences from the declaration which we were finally able to put together in that setting, under the influence of that spiritual clarity and speaking as Christians out of the three worlds:

> We are confronted in the world by a culture of violence concentrated in the Industrial States that with spreading tentacles is shaping the planet as a whole. This is evident in the military securing of peace through the system of deterrence, stockpiled with means of mass destruction.
>
> Thus at this moment when human being has taken total control of the world, we are faced with widespread world-negation and necrophilia which are difficult to interpret, and with nihilism in action.
>
> In all these phenomena we find sin and guilt. Both are repressed in the consciousness. An 'incapacity for grief' in turn produces insecurity, anxiety, *longing* for security, aggressiveness, and the projection of enemy images.

(May I insert here, in parentheses, a small note of homage to the German language. Being less influenced by Latin than English, the German speech has a way of showing the very picture of what is intended with the word itself. Enemy images: *Feindbilder!* How important are *Feindbilder* to every empire and would-be empire. The reason is obvious: human pretentions to power and glory are never fully believable all by themselves. So you must create the impression, if you want your ideology to be believed and fought for, that it is under attack by some enemy. This is why George Orwell in *1984* depicted that society as being perpetually at war. Big Brother will only be taken seriously if he is cast in the role of the Protector against some mythic foe. Every one of us who came to maturity during World War II were conditioned to think of Germans as compassionless, blond beasts and Japanese as small, green-yellow, almost ant-like creatures, ready to commit suicide for their cause. Today the world is full of whole industries that keep "images of the enemy" before the public. No one nation, people, or world has a monopoly on this game, though some may be more adept at it than others. It ought to give Christians considerable pause for thought in the light of our Lord's commandment to love your enemy. What might we not accomplish, if we took seriously our catholic, i.e. our ecumenical, character as Christ's Church, by way of offsetting this practice of *Feindbilder*-creation? It is a matter of ordinary human experience that human beings, when they are actually known, are always more complex and more mysterious than our graven images of them. How many Russians, for example, have our people—have we ourselves—known? The Russians whom I have met, both in person and in literature, hardly fit the *Feindbilder* that emanate from official and public sources in the Western World).[4]

The statement goes on to ask how, as Christians, representative of the traditions of Luther and Calvin, we might "speak to this situation":

Both traditions [Lutheran and Reformed] in essence testify to God's Yes to the world, that is, to a world which has become radically questionable and 'lost.' This Yes finds its central expression in the incarnation, the cross, and the resurrection of Christ.

God's Yes to the world is not only God's first, but also God's last word. Thus history with all its crises moves into the light of the coming kingdom of God. . . .Eschatological hope offers a foundation for the transformation of unjust conditions and the correction of deadly developments. Eschatological hope is able to save us from a glorification as well as a demonization of history.

God's yes to the world. God's covenant with life: this is the basis of our mission, the presupposition without which our stewardship of life lacks any horizon beyond our own wishful thinking. We are being commanded by historical providence today to take this very earnestly, even when it goes against the grain of our natural desire not to get involved, not to protest, not to follow in the train of our *protest*ant forebears and take up the cause of life against death.

3 On Swimming Against the Stream

But we should not jump to the conclusion that such an articulation of the gospel is either self-evident or easy. There are many drawbacks even to the theological expression of the gospel in terms of its life-affirmation, to say nothing about the actual *living* of such a gospel. One of the drawbacks is the Christian tradition itself. At Erfurt we bravely declared that both of our Protestant heroes, Luther and Calvin, had God saying a clear yes to the world in Jesus Christ. And I think that, in balance, this is true. But it is not as unambiguous as it might be. If not Luther and Calvin, then certainly some of their hangers-on were frequently given to world-weariness, had, like the disciples in *Jesus Christ Superstar*, "heaven on their minds." Escape-hatch religion, or should one say fallout-shelter religion, has been no stranger to the Protestant spirit. And so often, where the Christian tradition is not forthrightly world-negating, it has been at least highly ambiguous, hesitant, or docetic in relation to this world. "This is the highest wisdom," writes Thomas à Kempis in one of the most popular Christian devotional books of all ages: "This is the *highest* wisdom: to despise the world and aim at the kingdom of Heaven."[5] Reading so much of the literature of Christian piety and liturgy many, like the great Jewish author Elie Wiesel,[6] have concluded that Christians must be "half in love with easeful death." Against the hoary background of otherworldly longing and this-worldly complaint that accounts for so much of historical Christian piety, it is no easy thing even at the theological level to affirm credibly and with conviction that the gospel is God's covenant with life, and that the redemption and wholeness it seeks includes the healing of creation. It is not necessary to say that salvation is *only* an historical category; but we must learn, surely, how to speak of salvation as *also* an historical category. In fact I should claim that unless we can learn how to apply salvation *to the creation and to history* we shall have betrayed the gospel in our time. For as we have seen, we are living at a time of great world-weariness, cynicism, nihilism and necrophilia. The human being seems scarcely capable of mustering the courage and imagination necessary for its own self-preservation, supposedly the strongest instinct of all animate life. In such an historical moment it is necessary to swim against the stream. And swimming against the stream means affirming the world, affirming life, affirming and celebrating the creation. We must affirm life not in a mindless, dionysian way, not just a silly repetition of that favorite game of the 1960's, the *Age of Aquarius*, but in the full awareness of the power and the fascination of death, and in the shadow of the cross of Jesus Christ. If we transfer the salvific process to the suprahistorical sphere, as has been the wont of historic Christianity, then we betray that cross. The faith of the incarnation does not permit us to indulge in historical cynicism in the name of suprahistorical optimism, for our God has entered the lists of history's struggles; and the faith of the cross does not permit us to turn away from earth towards heaven, because the love of God is planted here in earth. It is as firmly planted here as was that cross on Golgotha. The theology of the cross is a way of speaking about God's abiding commitment to the earth; to abandon the world prematurely, as Bonhoeffer put it, it is a very antithesis of the theology of the cross.[7]

4 Spelling Out God's Covenant With Life

The God of Sinai and of Golgotha has made a covenant with life. But what does this mean concretely? The prophet Hosea answers that question in terms that are astonishingly contemporary:

> And I will make for you a covenant on that day . . . (1) with the beasts of the field, the birds of the air, and the creeping things of the ground; (2) and I will abolish the bow and the sword, and war, from the land, and will make you lie down in safety; (3) and I will betroth you to myself in righteousness and in justice . . .

Three aspects of the covenant God has made with life: a new theology of nature; a new theology of peace; and a new theology of justice. These are the very themes that occupy so much of our present-day thinking in the church.

First, God's covenant with life means God's affirmation of the whole of creation, and it implies a very definitive theology of nature. Hosea in fact possesses an ecological sense that is worthy of the best contemporary environmentalists. *There can be no covenant with humanity alone or exclusively.* Hosea accepts, of course, the general Hebraic assumption (surely a sound one) that the human creature has a central place in the scheme of things. The life of the world is dependent for its quality upon this speaking animal. The Hebrew prophet is not so romantic about nature as to assume that humankind's role is only to be and let be. "I will make *for you* a covenant with the beasts, the birds, the creeping things . . . " But for all the centrality of the human creature in the realm of creation, the prophet knows that humankind cannot stand alone and that God's affirmation of life must therefore recapitulate, in the new covenant, the creational patterns already seen by the ancient writers of Genesis. Like the eschatological vision of the Apocalypse of St. John, this poetic statement of new convenantal affirmation of created life pictures the coming to be of a wondrous harmony between all the species—a harmony not of human making; a harmony to which the human creature can contribute its special grace and glory, its leadership, only when it honors God's covenant with the other creatures. Critics of the biblical view of the relation between human and nonhuman nature are always noting cleverly that the God of the Bible gives humanity complete mastery over the other creatures, thus opening the door to the 20th century's ecological and resource and other natural crises. But in the passage from Hosea (and parallels can be found elsewhere in Scripture) the covenant that God makes, while it is for you—for the human community—is made with the nonhuman creatures. They have, as it were, their own arrangements with Management; they do not have to bargain with middle-management. To put it in more respectable, doctrinal language: nature (as we somewhat presumptuously designate all that is not ourselves) has in the biblical perspective an independent worth; it is not simply at human disposal. In the stewarding of nature, the terms are set not only by our own human need and greed but by the creaturely standing—status—of the other creatures, whose laws of being are not always commensurate with our designs upon them. We may *not* do whatever we please in the natural universe. There are limits. And when these limits are transgressed, it is not only that we are overstepping our authority vis-a-vis nature, we are transgressing God's very covenant with life; and we know, by now, the consequences of that transgression.

Second, the divine affirmation of the *life* of the world means the inauguration of *peace*. "I will abolish the bow (strong language) . . . I will make you lie down in safety." Recently I have had to do a good deal of thinking about violence. Does Christianity condone violence? . . .ever? Are there circumstances where violence is appropriate? In guerilla warfare for example, against oppressive military or economic forces? What about the continuing talk of a just war in the name of the Christian faith?

There is of course no easy answer to specific situational problems of Christian ethics. An *absolutist* pacifism not only begs many practical questions, but it raises the deeply theological question whether its advocates have not substituted the principle of peace for the living God. I do not believe in peace: I believe in God! Believing in God means obeying God in the concrete and always changing situations of real life, and real life never seems to present us with *absolutely* nonviolent alternatives. Indeed, the absolute advocacy of peace, as Rudy Wiebe has poignantly shown in his brilliant first novel, *Peace Shall Destroy Many*, can unintentionally erupt into the most terrifying violence.

There can however be no doubt, surely, that the *will* of God in the biblical tradition from first to last is that there should be peace, not just the absence of hostilities, but peace—shalom! Peace with righteousness, justice! Even violence, where it is tolerated or (on occasion) even commanded in the Scriptures is justifiable only as a possible means of restoring some approximation of shalom in an imperfect and sinful world. There is a deep skepticism throughout the Bible about any attempt to establish a principle in which it could be demonstrated that violence can contribute to ultimate peace. If there is a principle in Scripture (and the Scriptures are rightly careful about principles of every sort) it is more nearly that violence begets violence: those who take up the sword perish by the sword (see Matthew 26:52). The God who says yes to life must say no to war as this God does in Hosea. And it does not qualify that point in the least to remind us that the God of the Bible sometimes actually leads God's people into battle. Because the God of the Scriptures does many things that do not belong to God's *essence*. Life is an intensely complicated affair, even for God! Like every parent, the Parent of us all must frequently engage in activities and issue counsel that goes against the grain of what is clearly the biblical God's *will* and *intention*. We may put this down to anthropomorphism if we will, but the alternative to the very human God of the Scriptures[9] is a remote and principled Deity who could not love. I for one am glad to settle for the humanity of God in this respect. Apart from simply overwhelming human freedom and dignity in some kind of superbehaviorist way, God, like any loving parent, inevitably becomes enmeshed in the ambiguities of human history. I know that as a father I must do and say many things that, I fervently hope, my children will one day, if not already today, realize do not belong to my essential nature. Fortunately, I think that my four children do in fact understand that I am somehow different from some of the things that I do, that I am not to be equated, simply, with my deeds and my words.

Israel at its best always understood this about its God. We remember that the God of Israel allowed the sea to swallow up those who were pursuing God's people to bring them back into slavery. But then, in the beautiful midrash, God is found weeping while delivered Israel celebrates its crossing of the Red Sea. Why does God weep while God's people rejoice? Because . . . "I am weeping for my children, the Egyptians."

We remember, too, that the God of Israel can even contemplate the destruction of the creation, its goodness notwithstanding. But unlike Hal Lindsey's god, the God of Israel backs away in horror from the sick logic that suggests (if we may borrow words from the war in Southeast Asia) that God may have to destroy the creation in order to save it. Since death for the tradition of Jerusalem is not only a physical but also a spiritual category, the God of the Great Flood, parent-like, must resort to the infliction of physical death to prevent the more terrible plague of a spiritual death that is carrying the whole creation towards the gates of doom. But even in that ancient saga, where the biblical tradition perhaps comes nearest to the concept of salvation through destruction, the aim of the God of Noah and all the creatures is not, finally, the demolition of creation but its life in the face of a ubiquitous, self-chosen form of death.

In other words, we do not have to pass over the difficult, paradoxical dimension of God's struggle with death—yes, *God's own struggle* to sustain creation in life. It is believable, this biblical account of God's struggle for the life of creation, precisely because it is not easy. Death is taken very seriously. This is no fairy tale in which it is obvious from the beginning that light will win over darkness, good over evil, the divine over the demonic, life over death. There were blood, sweat and tears in Golgotha. For that which negates life is very real. But there is no doubt about the end-principle that informs this story from first to last: it is life, not death. It is peace, not war. It is plowshares, not swords. The God who makes a covenant with life, a costly covenant, written in the *life*-blood of a Just Man, is a God whose face is set against bloodshed. How much more is God's face set against a war that itself *could* constitute the very ultimate destruction that God will not permit God's own omnipotence to entertain.

Third, Hosea's God, in making this covenant with life, insists upon righteousness, justice: "And I will betroth you to myself in righteousness and in justice . . . "

There are many today who long for peace; and there are also many who work for a new respect on the part of the human element for nonhuman nature. In our First World particularly these objectives can consume our energies so totally that we neglect the injustice and inequality that are at the same time the presupposition and the outcome of these other ills. It is instructive to listen to the confessions of Christians in exploited parts of the world as they engage today, along with us, in their attempts at geocentrizing the gospel, at bringing the gospel back to earth. They do not neglect peace, certainly; nor do they overlook ecology though their treatment of the natural order tends to be much less romantic than ours. But through all of their theology there runs a concern for justice, including economic justice. This is, I fear, so foreign to our First World churches that we, along with the leaders of our nations, are tempted to write it off as being Marxist-inspired. But it is not inspired by Karl Marx alone. Karl Marx himself was not inspired by Karl Marx alone. He was not a son of Israel for nothing. The concern for every form of justice, including economic justice, permeates the prophetic tradition of Israel, and it was certainly inherited by that other son of Israel who was annointed to preach good news to the poor.

One of the best corporate examples that I know of the concern for justice emanating today from the Third World is the "Confession of Faith" issued in 1978 by the Presbyterian-Reformed Church in Cuba. A few paragraphs from this confession will illustrate my point:

> In the historic realization of the Revelation in Jesus Christ, God does not graze in a tangential way the concrete reality of the human being, but rather, on the contrary, he inserts himself in History, taking it on as His own. In that way He calls us all to fulfill ourselves as human beings through concrete historical projects of redemption . . .

> When the Church lives its love for "Jesus Christ and him crucified," it takes on in full responsibility the solution presented by God to the human problem through sacrificial and solidary love which works justice and establishes peace.

> The Scriptures teach us that the human being is characterized by being an 'econome' of all things—God's *steward*. All goods, material and spiritual, that we obtain as persons or as nations, cannot be considered in the final analysis as 'individual' or 'national' property in an exclusive way, be it individualistic, classist, elitist, or nationalistic. Much less can they have a transcendent value which, by reason of the 'natural law' or 'divine law,' has been given goods as private ownership of the means of production.

> To make human spirituality essentially dependent on the exercising of the so-called 'right to private property' constitutes one of the most tragic aberrations . . . that human spirituality has suffered to this day . . .

> The Church proclaims that the human vocation is that of being a 'good econome.' The 'house' (oikos) that the human creature administers is the whole world of Creation; and each person is responsible for it to his fellow-creatures and to God.

> The Church teaches that the committed participation of its members in public life, in the administration of its economy, is not something one can choose to add or not to add to his condition as believer; on the contrary, the responsible exercise of this right is an integral and inseparable part of the loving practice of the Christian faith.[10]

Our sisters and brothers in the Third World, and in pockets of our own as well, are being impelled by the same gospel as we, the gospel of God's gracious and intensive commitment to creation. They are telling us that this same process of returning the gospel to earth has implications for justice, for a righteousness and faithfulness that are often hard for us to hear about. But if we are serious about exploring a Christian mission that has as its foundational presupposition God's covenant with life in the kingdom of death, we cannot stop in our reflection upon this theo-logic where it is still less than personally painful to us. The God who wants to save us for life wants to save us, not only from the death that others are inflicting upon our world, but also from the death whose infrastructures we ourselves support, contribute to, and benefit from. In a real sense, the acid test of our sincerity in this process of reinterpreting the gospel as God's covenant with life is whether we Christians of the First World are able and willing to adjust our own lifestyles to the claims for justice and righteousness coming to us from those who are being done to death by our way of life.

DIALOGUE

Question: I like what you said about God's judgment—that it's for the *cleansing* of the world. Do you think *we* are being judged—I mean, America? . . . maybe the whole First World?

Response: If we insist on comparing ourselves with ancient Israel (and on this continent we've been doing that ever since Europeans settled here), then we had better be prepared to be judged, because that's what the God of Israel was always doing to Israel. "You only of all the peoples of the earth have I known, therefore I will punish you for all your iniquities." (Amos 3:2)

Judgment belongs to the biblical understanding of the divine *love*. You can't have the one without the other. The whole First World is a highly privileged world, and none is so privileged in it as are the two northern nations of this continent. I suspect that we shall have to experience a good deal of humiliation in the future, perhaps in the next century. We can no longer escape the guilty knowledge that our prosperity is dependent upon keeping other peoples poor, oppressed and afraid.

But there is one important thing about God's judgment that is frequently overlooked by the faithful: namely, God gives God's people the opportunity of *participating* in God's own judgment of them. Concretely, this means that if we are willing, we can already engage in the kind of self-analysis and self-criticism that might bring about changes in our expectations and our ways of doing things—changes that could even avert the worst aspects of the judgment under which we stand. That's why the prophetic community of faith has to point to the critical aspects of our corporate life (by the way, the English words crisis and critical come directly from the Greek word for judgement: *krisis*). Prophetic faith does not remind people of their guilt and the dangers they are courting just to be critical (in the popular sense of the term), but so that through participation in God's *krisis* we can change (repent!) before we have reached the point of no return.

Question: Excuse me if I am blunt, but I was rather shocked by your insinuation that the state might be the mouthpiece of, well, of the devil. Or at least not God. Didn't St. Paul say we should obey the "ruling authorities" because "they have their power from God"? And didn't Martin Luther say that the state was "the left arm of God"? Something like that, anyway?

Response: Yes . . . unfortunately! I suspect that if St. Paul had known how his advice in Romans 13 might be used by dictators and others to justify so many horrendous deeds he would have cut off his right hand before penning that particular line. As for Luther, we should not forget that he had the responsibility of building up the authority of the little provincial German states against the enormous power of the Holy Roman Empire and the Church. He was not speaking within the political context of a great empire like the U.S.A. today, but in the tiny land of Saxony.

But listen: this isn't the only kind of counsel you can get from the Bible or from Christian tradition. John Knox said that if the ruler is opposing God's will, then the ruler him/herself must be opposed, and strongly so. As for the Scriptures, they are by no means as beholden to earthly powers as St. Paul in Romans 13 proposes. If the Bible itself does not hesitate to suggest that kings and leaders of Israel are frequently led astray, or become tyrants worthy of death (Ahab and Jezebel, for instance); if it doesn't hesitate even to criticize its own greatest hero, King David, why should we present the Christian faith as a religion that always vouches for the goodness and authenticity of whatever power comes our way? Under the influence precisely of Paul and Luther (to name only two authorities), millions of Germans in the 1930's were ready to welcome Adolf Hitler as God's own representative and "left arm." Even Hitler's race policies didn't alert them to the demonic character of his intentions. To believe in the sole glory and authority of God, however, is surely to be vigilant, always, for those who bear authority in our midst. Authority is necessary to human community. But it is also a great temptation. If only God's authority is ultimate, then every other authority is purely relative, and must be measured by the canon of God's authority, which is the authority of suffering love (agape).

Question: I guess you must have heard me chuckle when you said "Pro*test*ant with the emphasis on the second syllable, I mean. Did you do that on purpose? I had the feeling you probably did.

Response: Of course! It might do us a lot of good. Maybe it would eventually give us a new identity altogether if we old, staid, civilized *Pro*testants began to call ourselves Pro*test*ants. That's why we got the name in the first place, you know, because we are pro*test*ing something. The "Protestant Principle," the very thing that makes protestants protestants, according to Paul Tillich, is the refusal to give anything less than the Ultimate the status of the ultimate: for instance (see the question above) to regard earthly rulers of state or church as if they were direct mouthpieces of the Divine, or to confuse ultimate truth with some time-conditioned expression of truth. If we really carried on in this Reformation tradition, fewer of us would blanch at marching with the protestors, maybe.

Question: What do you mean when you say Christianity has been "docetic" in relation to the world? Sorry, I just don't understand this term.

Response: I'm sorry too—for using too much technical language. But in a way we all have to become theologians today, so your question becomes an occasion to learn this important term out of our past.

The word docetic comes from a Greek verb, *dokeō,* which means to seem or to appear. It was used by some early Christians to explain the humanity of Jesus. They didn't want to confess that he was *really* human; they wanted him to be *essentially* divine. So they said that he only *appeared to be* human: the flesh (incarnation) was an appearance.

So the term docetic is often applied to versions of the Christian faith that stress the spiritual side—not only of Jesus but of everything related to belief. For instance docetic-minded believers often look upon everything material (including of course the body) as being the source of our human problems; accordingly, they find salvation in an escape from "the world and the flesh," which they more or less equate with the third noun in that familiar phrase, "the devil." We have this kind of emphasis in Christianity on account of our early associations with Hellenistic religion and culture, which characteristically downgraded matter. It is not an Hebraic sentiment.

Question: I find myself wanting to agree with you that we have to understand salvation as an historical process, but I'm afraid of becoming utopian. You have referred to Reinhold Niebuhr from time to time, and one of his criticisms of modern Christianity was exactly its utopianism. He wanted us to be "Christian realists." Aren't you asking us to return to a new utopianism?

Response: As you know, Professor Niebuhr was one of my own teachers, and the theologian of our immediate past whom I respect most, in many ways. So your question seems to me a serious one. But I would like to make two observations:

First, while Dr. Niebuhr was critical of utopianism and urged Christians to be realists, this never led him personally to a passive acceptance of the status quo. More than perhaps anyone in his generation, he strove for what he called "proximate goals."

We can't turn earth into heaven, but we can make it a better earth. Unfortunately some of those who learned from him about the ambiguity of all historical effort did not learn this other lesson, namely, that we are nevertheless responsible, as Christians, for effecting what changes we can.

Secondly, we have to recognize that Professor Niebuhr did his work under certain historical circumstances. The situation he had to address, especially in his earlier and most formative years, was not quite the same as our present day situation. What he had most to battle in those days was the influence of Liberalism, with its religion of historical progress and its naivety about evil and sin. We live in an age that still uses the language of idealism at the rhetorical level, but manifests an underside of cynicism and fatalism. I suspect that if Dr. Niebuhr were alive today he would accent the lesson he always taught us about "changing the things that can be changed." If you consider the three categories referred to in the prayer that he wrote, the famous prayer that was adopted by Alcoholics Anonymous and other groups, you can detect this as one of the important emphases of his thought:

> Give me the *serenity* to accept what cannot be changed,
> the *courage* to change what can be changed, and
> the *wisdom* to know the difference between them.

The Christian always prays for wisdom of that kind; but there are times when the serenity of acceptance has to be accented, and there are other times when the courage to change is more appropriate. That courage always requires some vision of what is possible to give it wings.

Question: On a number of occasions you have made reference to the theology of the cross. I assumed at first you were speaking about what is usually called the doctrine of the atonement, but I suspect you have something else in mind. Could you speak to this?

Response: The theology of the cross (*theologia crucis*) was a term invented by Martin Luther, but it points to a whole way of thinking about Christian faith that is older than Luther. I would say it has its roots in the religion of Israel. To understand what Luther meant by it, you have to realize what he was fighting against. He named the position over against which he developed his *theologia crucis* "the theology of glory" (*theololgia gloriae*). Today we might call it religious triumphalism or the religion of success. The theology of glory always stresses what it likes to regard as the positive aspects of the Christian story: the triumph of the Christ over all his enemies, and here-and-now fulfilment of the Christian life in happy and successful living, the glory of the Church, the power of God, etc. Luther felt that such an approach to the gospel not only ignored the cross, which Paul said stands at the center of our faith (I Corinthians 1 and 2), but that it leads to a false, theoretical victory that doesn't jibe with the real world. The world as it is is full of suffering and pain; the life of faith, too, is a matter of an ongoing struggle with doubt and darkness. So when we give ourselves emotionally and intellectually to a gospel in which everything has been set right already, we not only falsify existence but we inevitably cut ourselves off from those who are most obviously caught in situations of oppression.

Therefore, Luther thought, we have to learn how to perceive the victory of the Christ "hidden beneath its opposite," that is, not as an obvious triumph, comparable to Caesar's victories or the success of this world's VIPs, but as another kind of victory altogether. God's way of winning (if you even want to use that language) is utterly different from Caesar's in that it looks for all the world like losing. From this world's point of view, Jesus the crucified is one of history's losers. And that's just why all the losers can find in him a friend. And . . . are there, finally, any *winners*, Caesar-style?

Question: Do you really think there is any way of changing Western attitudes towards nature? Aren't we so entrenched in a mentality of lording it over the rest of creation that we will never learn how to live with the other creatures?

Response: On my bad days I suspect what you are saying is the only truth. Maybe we have already gone so far towards the mastering of the natural universe that we will soon inherit an uninhabitable biosphere. There's an old expression—"being hoist with your own petard." A petard was a metal cone filled with explosives and fixed to walls or fortress doors in the warfare of the past. Sometimes the people who rigged the petard to the enemy fortress got blown up in the process. It looks to many people today as if this is the kind of collision course Western technocratic society is on. When you start out to control nature, you forget that you are part of the nature that you intend to control. If we don't blow ourselves up with the most ingenious of our technological inventions (i.e., our weapons of warfare), perhaps we'll end in some sort of B.F. Skinner-like behaviorism where everybody is programmed to do the right thing. In either case, we'll have carried to its most logical conclusion the lording-it-over nature mentality.

But while we should not underestimate the prospects of such a scenario (we have to be Christian realists), neither can we resignedly assume that humanity is simply locked into this kind of pattern. All over the world today, especially in the so-called First World, there are people who are saying no to the technocratic mentality. Most of them are ordinary people, humanists, idealists, socialists, concerned scientists, and even technologists; and if we listen to them they are telling us something about our own *Christian* tradition that many Christians have forgotten or never knew. The terms steward or stewardship are very often included in their messages to us. For instance, a noted philosopher of the University of Michigan, Henryk' Skolimowski, in a book widely read in the scientific community, writes that the only alternative to the post-industrial society that is courting doom is the conscious development of what he calls "Ecological Humanism"; and the first principle of such humanism, as he states it, is this: *"The coming age is to be seen as the age of stewardship: we are here not to govern and exploit, but to maintain and creatively transform, and to carry on the torch of evolution."* (The italics are his.)

Sometime I think it is literally true what Jesus said in the newer Testament: "If the children are silent, the stones will cry out." If the Christians are silent, the philosophers and scientists and humanists will cry out. Today the world itself is catechizing us about the meaning of our own gospel.

Question: I'm confused. Everything you say points to pacifism, and yet you announced just now, "I do not believe in pacifism." Am I hearing double-think (to quote Orwell)?

Response: I wouldn't say so. It seems to me a very important distinction, in fact. What I said was: I do not believe in pacifism, I believe in God. The key term is "believe in." When people say that they believe in pacifism (or in any other *ism*, for that matter) then, if they are being serious about it, they mean that they are putting their trust in a certain system of thought, set of ideas, propositions, principles, theories, ethical precepts or what have you. I don't think this is an option for Christians. Christians do not believe in ideas or systems, but in God. God cannot be reduced to principles or theories, not even to good doctrinal or theological theories. God is a living god—Thou! If I turn God into a set of ideas or principles I have substituted for the living God something fixed, static, an It, not a Thou. As Person, God interacts with persons, responding to the changing circumstances of our lives as individuals and communities. God's word for us as teenagers setting out in the world may be quite different from God's word for us as septugenarians. God's command to a people oppressed by an exploitative empire will certainly be quite different from God's word to that empire. The question that faith asks is not, How can I be consistent with my theory, my moral code, my theological doctrine?, but rather,

How can I be obedient to God here and now?

It is my opinion that in the nuclear age, and as a member of a First World society (an oppressing society), God's word to me is, "Strive for peace, resist the arms race, negotiate with those perceived as the enemy, etc." But I cannot turn this word into an *absolute* that would be applicable to everybody everywhere, including my counterparts in Third World nations who are victims of my world's oppressive economic and other policies. Obviously I do think it is God's command to all of us who belong to the *have* nations in which (not incidentally) the nuclear threat is greatest to become nuclear pacifists. But I am not prepared to make pacifism a universal Christian absolute, and thus exclude from faith some whose struggle for justice may involve them in local conflict.

Question: I was intrigued by your idea that God has to do things that do not belong to God's essence, as you put it. I had not thought of that before and it helps to explain many questions that have puzzled me, especially in biblical stories where God is pictured as being angry, or wrathful, or vengeful or apparently arbitrary, etc. But wouldn't it be possible to carry this too far? I mean, surely there must be some sort of consistency between God's essence and what God actually does. Otherwise you present a God who is lacking in integrity.

Response: I greatly sympathize with your concern. But I wonder: If the one thing you want to be really consistent about is loving someone, is it not likely that your behavior will seem to be inconsistent, at least to onlookers?

As I interpret it, the God of the Scriptures is motivated by one intention predominantly: to love the creature. This applies to both testaments. It does not mean that God is indifferent about other qualities—such as justice, truth, holiness, integrity, fairness, fidelity, etc. But what dominates the biblical picture of God is God's loving involvement with creation, especially the human creature. And the *kind* of consistency that belongs to love is different from the consistency that belongs to other qualities I have just named. To be consistently truthful, for instance, you simply have to bind yourself to the principle of truth (well, it isn't simple, of course, far from it). It's a different thing from consistently loving, however. Because with love what you have bound yourself to (even if you are God!) is not an ethical principle (Tell the truth!) but a living being. And this being won't stand still and just be loved in the same way each day, with all the same gestures and words and little ceremonials repeated without variation. This being keeps moving about and changing, one day this, one day that. To be a really consistent lover you have to adjust all the time to the changing circumstances of the beloved. One day you have to be gentle and the next resolute, here forgiving, there firm, now direct, then indirect, etc. We are not talking about tolerance, after all, but love. If I love my child I am going to be very responsive to my child, trying to find the right response to exactly what is going on then and there. And since what is going on in the child's life is not something altogether predictable but full of nuances and transitions and varying moods, my responses are going to seem, to the onlooker, lacking in any conspicuous or principalled consistency. But I will know, and eventually the child will also know, that all the perhaps chaotic variety of my behavior towards it was woven into a tapestry of consistency by the one great motif: my intention to love it well.

The God of the Scriptures has, if you will, a kind of handicap by comparison with other sorts of gods that have been conceived by human beings, especially the wonderful, reasonable gods of the philosophers. Our God's handicap is love, rightly called *hesed* and *agape*, i.e. faithful and suffering love. This love gets God into a great deal of trouble, so far as other virtues (such as reasonableness, omnipotence, impassability, immutability, things theologians are always assigning to Deity) are concerned. If God did not love, God could be wonderfully rational, even cool! God could be absolutely unchanging (immutable), if only God would keep at a safe distance from the world, aloof, untouched. But since God, according to the tradition of Jerusalem, does love, God like every other real lover has frequently to sacrifice integrity for the sake of the beloved. And by the way, our tradition claims not only that God does love, but that "God is love": love is God's essence.

Question: Towards the end of your meditation, you used the term "geocentrizing" the gospel. What's behind that?

Response: What's behind it are centuries of presenting the gospel as if it were meant for heaven and not earth. The good news is first of all the announcement of God's *earthly* advent, God's presence "with us" (Emmanuel). Religion, which you remember we distinguished, earlier, from faith, is always trying to get God back up into heaven: up there and out there as Bishop Robinson put it. Faith on the contrary attempts to respond to God's active presence among us. A theology that is in the service of the community of faith, and not just a religious or scholastic exercise, has always to attempt to demonstrate the essentially earthward orientation of the God who is its primary concern. Because it is theocentric and Christocentric it has to be *geo*centric (centered in earth), because that's where its *Theos* and its *Christos* are centered.

THE MANDATE OF OUR MISSION: STEWARDSHIP OF LIFE

Introduction and Recapitulation

Let me recapitulate: In the First Meditation I drew attention to the confusion that surrounds the question of the Christian mission today. Our experience of religious pluralism, the historically conditioned character of truth, and the limitations and dangers of religious triumphalism, among other things, has severed us from conventional conceptions of Christian mission; yet we seem not to have discovered convincing alternatives to those conventions. Meantime, the world in which we live has evolved in ways hardly anticipated by our own optimistic forebears on this continent; and I suggested that if we meditate with sufficient imagination and seriousness upon the threatening conditions in which as a civilization we find ourselves, we Christians could discover a new (though not novel) way of conceiving of our mission. In a world whose life is gravely jeopardized, the vocation to which Christians are called is the stewardship of life.

The four subsequent meditations are simply an attempt to explore that hypothesis in greater detail.

Thus in the Second Meditation we reflected upon "The Context of Our Mission" as one in which the leading classes and structures of society have made, in Isaiah's phrase, "a covenant with death." Barbara Tuchman has suggested[1] that the closest historical parallel to our present situation could be the 14th century: the breakdown of the Medieval World. The fifth century of the Common Era—the final capitulation of the Roman Empire to the barbarians—is perhaps another period mirroring our own in certain ways. St Augustine and his contemporaries did their theology and lived their Christian witness in the midst of that societal disintegration and cultural decay. As Augustine lay dying in 430 A.D. the barbarian hordes were sacking his city of Hippo. The disintegration of our own society has also been seen

by many in what has been called "the epidemic of violence"—
by which they refer not only to the violence of the nations in
their dealings with one another, but also the violence of our
cities, our highways, and so many private lives. The major causes
of the death of males between 18 and 30 years of age in the
United States today, I am informed, are in this order: automobile
accidents, suicide, murder, and cancer. As 80 to 90 percent of
cancer is caused by environmental factors, this fourth cause of
mortality betokens yet another face of our malaise: the lethal
side of the age of high technology. A commentator on the decline of Rome wrote that the greatest evidence of that historic
decline and fall was not such obvious degradation as open
violence, however, but the faces of the leading citizens. We can
still see these faces in what was probably their actual state,
slightly beautified; for busts of those citizens, who loved to have
themselves sculpted, populate every major museum in the world.
They are, said a famous art historian, the faces of persons who
no longer expect anything. One is reminded of the title of
Christopher Lasch's best-selling book, *The Culture of Narcissism: America in an Age of Diminishing Expectations.*[2] This
is the context of our mission!

In the Third Meditation we reflected on the *basis* of our mission. I said that one of the salutory consequences of the sort
of death-courting circumstances in which as Christians we find
ourselves today is that we have begun to discover, by way of
contrast so to speak, that the gospel we have been called to announce is at its very core life- and world-affirming. Against this
contextual backdrop of apathy, cynicism, escapism and
necrophilia, there is among us (it seems to me) a growing con-
sensus that the Christian message is at base a statement about
the essential *goodness* of creation and its healing. Without being romantic or pollyanna about the world, its limitations, its
potential and actual evil, darkness and sin—in fact from a point
at the very center of that darkness (the cross of Golgotha!)—
the Christian gospel celebrates life and proclaims that the
Creator of the world has set in motion, in history, a process and
mystery of redemption. The empirical church of the past has
often, and perhaps characteristically, flirted with world rejection, and it has presented salvation as a way of getting out of
this world. But today we have seen that such an interpretation
of the Christian message simply plays into the hands of the
forces in our world that are already courting oblivion. In the face
of our world's pursuit of a manifold death, we are helped to discover at last that the gospel of Jesus as the Christ is nothing
more and nothing less than God's new covenant with *life*. That
covenant is the *basis* of our mission.

Now, given such a *context* on the one hand, and such a *basis* for our mission on the other, we are to ask at this point: What is the *mandate* of our mission? What is the nature of the commandment, the commission, under which as disciples of the Christ we find ourselves in this historical moment? The Deuteronomist, to whom I turn for the scriptural background of this *Fourth Meditation*, could be a contemporary prophet—with a doctorate in sociology as well as theology.

"See, I have set before you this day life and good, death and evil. If you obey the commandments of the Lord your God which I command you this day, by loving the Lord your God, by walking in his ways, and by keeping his commandments and his statutes and his ordinances, then you shall live and multiply, and the Lord your God will bless you in the land which you are entering to take possession of it. But if your heart turns away, and you will not hear, but are drawn away to worship other gods and serve them, I declare to you this day, that you shall perish; you shall not live long in the land which you are going over the Jordan to enter and possess. I call heaven and earth to witness against you this day, that I have set before you life and death, blessing and curse; therefore choose life, that you and your descendants may live, loving the Lord your God, obeying his voice, and cleaving to him . . . "
—*Deuteronomy 30:15–20a*

1 The Gospel: Life Is There for the Choosing

Choose life! That, in two words, is the mandate of our mission. It is at once a matter of gospel and of law, of possibility and commandment.

It is gospel because our choice of life does not have to be some idealistic work of our own, grasping after utopia in the name of some ideology or other, taking heaven by storm. It is precisely what the Reformers said it was: *sola gratia*. Sheer grace! We *may* choose life—it's a matter of permission, not a pipe dream—because our God had already chosen life. This basis must never be overlooked as we turn to the question of our mandate. God has covenanted (as Hosea put it) with all God's creatures in our behalf. Or to remind ourselves of the newer Testament's witness to the costly nature of the grace that is the basis of our mission, let us put it this way: through a personal encounter with death and the demonic, the God revealed in Jesus Christ has established for us a way through the impasse of everything that keeps us back from the promise of life. Through identification with us in our "journey towards death" (Heidegger), God has broken the hold of death upon life. Life is thus a real possibility for us, in spite of everything that seems to deny us access to life's fulness. Peace is possible. "Peace could break out!" (Sölle). A new relation between Homo sapiens and the other creatures of earth is possible. Justice is possible. These are not pie-in-the-sky promises, naive idealism, whistling in the dark, utopianism and all the other clever epithets thrown today at anyone who does not give in to the cynicism of those who have resigned themselves to the way of death. The self-styled "practical" people like to call that cynicism "realism." But the only practical people left, say Paul and Anne Ehrlich at the end of their long study of *Population, Resources and Environment,*[3] are "the visionaries who talk of love, beauty, peace, and plenty." To be a visionary you do not *have* to be stupid, or naive or innocent. Christian visionaries like Helder Camara and Jean Vanier and Mother Teresa are certainly not people who have shut their eyes to the antithesis of love, beauty, peace and plenty. I wager such persons know more about hatred, ugliness, war and want than do the comfortable academics and others who brand them "visionaries." To become one of the practical, practicing visionaries who are "the only realists left," all we Christians have to do is to believe and receive the grace that is offered us by the life-choosing God who speaks from Sinai and Golgotha. Even just to *begin* to believe, no great effort of faith is required; it could be no bigger than a mustard seed . . . and it will always be, certainly, in dialogue with doubt. But this much is clear: we are not asked to shut our eyes to all the degradation and death that negates the courage to believe in the God of life. Christians take their stand, after all, in the environs of Golgotha. But precisely there, in the midst of all that dying, injustice, and pathos of human vulnerability, the Camaras and Vaniers and Teresas of the Church perceive a great *in spite of.* They discover and rediscover, the more thay have to do with death, that God is on the side of life. Therefore death, with all its show of triumph and pomp, they affirm, does not rule this world. *Jesos Christos Kurios!* cried the earliest Christians; or rather, they whispered it while the crowd was shouting *Kaisar Kurios!* (Caeser is Lord!) And they had precious little of what our world counts hard evidence for their claim. But something about the very noisiness of the pomp and circumstance of that already-decadent Empire made them feel the courage of belief. We are mistaken—gravely mistaken!—if we think that faith comes easiest to those who are surrounded by blessings. The great confessions of the Church have always been evoked from those who stood in darkness and the shadow of death, like the little confessing Synod at Barmen in 1934, whose 50th anniversary we celebrate this year. And the reason for this is not very obscure, given the logic of the cross. For it is only when we can no longer pretend to rely upon our own resources, when we have rediscovered that "we are beggars" (Luther), that we can truly know that *we do not have to rely upon our own resources. Sola gratis!* Dying, we know that *life* is possible!

This experience belongs in a particular way to faith; but it is in some real measure also a possibility for all life, including the life of collectivities. For grace, as the Reformers knew when they wrote of "common grace," is not wholly discontinuous with nature; in fact, in a real way God's grace is the presupposition of all the workings of nature, and of history. Thus it is possible even for nations and civilizations to experience, at the eleventh hour, new possibilites, opportunities for renewal that are not logically commensurate with their past. At the very moment when World War II was taking shape in Europe, Reinhold Niebuhr was writing a footnote for the second volume of his Gifford Lectures, in which he said that . . .

> . . . In their glory, when the disintegration of evil is already apparent in their life and the ultimate destruction is so long postponed [the fate of societies] reveals the 'long suffering' of the divine mercy. For God's judgments are never precipitate and the possibilities of repentance and turning from the evil way are many. According to the degree with which civilizations and cultures accept these possibilities of renewal, they may extend their life indeterminately.[4]

We may choose life. The gift is given us individually, corporately. Life is there for the choosing.

2 The Law Within the Gospel

But this gospel comes to us as law, as a "radical imperative" (John Bennett). Niebuhr goes on in the same passage to say that *many* of the civilizations and cultures that may through repentance and turning extend their life "indeterminately" nevertheless "at some point or other . . . make the fatal mistake, or a whole series of fatal mistakes. Then they perish; and the divine majesty is vindicated in that destruction."[5]

Life is not going to go on all by itself, whether we choose it or reject it or simply refrain from any kind of decision. God's covenant with life is not for God's own sake but *pro nobis*—for us! Covenants in the Bible are two-way affairs, and this new covenant in the lifeblood of Jesus is no exception. God makes no promise to protect and preserve life *over against* the human decision that it is not worth protecting and preserving. It is a facile and unbiblical interpretation of the meaning of divine providence that assumes any such thing. As the better traditions of Calvinism have always known (and that may be their greatest contribution to Christian understanding), "There is a law within the gospel." The Deuteronomist (that good Calvinist!) states this tradition very precisely in our text: the *gospel* is that God has really made life possible—life, and good. The law within this gospel is that we are exhorted from our side to *choose* life and the good. We shall not truly have heard that gospel until we have also heard that law within it. Actively, in full consciousness, and in the face of great honesty about death and evil, *choose life!* Choose *the good!* You may do this. So do it!

Moreover, there is no neutral stance. You do not choose life merely by avoiding death, repressing your deep awareness of it, narcissistically cultivating a little world of private happiness. Not to choose is to choose: it is to choose death. We are challenged by the law within the gospel, not merely to cease being ambiguous about the world and the life of the world, but actually to confirm it, positively to embrace it, joyfully to celebrate it. We are commanded by this precious law of the gospel to treasure the creaturely life that has been offered to us at such a cost; to treat creation as a gift so precious that it requires sacrifice and restraint, on our part, so that we may in turn help to preserve it for future generations. For there is no obeying this Law of the Gospel of Life without personal sacrifice. And today that is not only a bit of Christian piety but a law of economics: If we do not alter, restrain ourselves, and simplify our style of life, our children will indeed reap the whirlwind. Other people's children already have! As Jonathan Schell has put it in one of those nonreligious studies of our time that turn out to be deeply religious: "Formerly the future was simply given to us; now it must be achieved."[6] Choose *life!*

3 Courage to Choose

We hesitate when we hear the commandment to decide for life. There is much within us that wills life. Our very bodies will opt for life even when our souls crave the forgetfulness of the long sleep. Yet we are conscious, too, of our own weakness, and of the enormity of the challenge that is issued by the gospel of life in a world whose patterns of self-destruction seem so intractable. Death is a power in our world. It is not just sham. Evil is real! Calvin may have understood better than Luther that there is a law within the gospel, but Luther understood better than Calvin that to become the hearer of this law is to be placed at the very crossroad between God and the devil. I mean that Luther's eschatololgy was more realistic. Like the author of Hebrews (2:8-9), Luther did not see everything put under the feet of the conquering Christ; rather, he saw the crucified One, whose victory is (as Luther put it) "hidden beneath its opposite." The power of death in the life of our world today obscures the life that God is giving to it through God's own subjection to death. There are things going on in the world that, if we permit ourselves to dwell on them with any seriousness, almost overwhelm us with grief and fear. To read the average newspaper today one has to have recourse to something like the long-since discarded terminology of the medieval Christians even to comprehend the motives behind the deeds that are recorded there. The Enlightenment's categories for describing the world, categories like progress and freedom and mastery—the concepts on which we (on this continent) have been reared—are too rational, too civilized, too positive to permit us even to glance in the general direction of the hell that our children and grandchildren are dreaming about and singing about in their strange, repetitive, seemingly mindless songs.

And we ask ourselves: What chance does an individual have in the face of all this? What chance even do whole movements and coalitions have against the powers of our technocratic and nuclear hell? Who can cry halt to the arms race? Who can stop the tide of spiritual death that is occurring in anticipation of the futureless future? Who can influence governments to put their budgets to *human* use, to cap the causes of acid rain, to channel aid that will enhance the *life* of nations in Central and South America? No! We should not underestimate the powers of darkness.

But listen again to our sociologist-prophet: "this commandment which I command you this day is not too hard for you, neither is it far off . . . " It is hard, but it is not too hard. It is not impossible—though if it were *only* commandment, only law, it would certainly be impossible. But the impossible becomes possible when God makes it God's possibility for us. And God has done that: has done it, is doing it, will do it. We live, as it has so often been said during this 20th century, "between the times," between an "already" and a "not yet."

Not yet! The old reality of death and evil is not ended, to be sure. In her profound little book, *The Arms Race Kills: Even Without War,* Dorothy Sölle tells of a political Lenten vigil arranged by her group in Cologne and announced under the theme, "It Is Not Finished." The theme caused a turmoil in that city, because many influential Christians saw the statement as a direct affront to the 'realized eschatology of our Lord's statement from the cross, "It is finished." But Sölle writes that if you turn Jesus' "It is finished" into a rigid ideology, you end up with a religion that is constitutionally incapable of taking in the seriousness of evil, and therefore incapable either of honesty, or compassion, or the determination to change the world.[7] We do not live on the other side of the Parousia, we live *Zwischen den Zeiten* (between the times): between the humiliation and the glorification of the Word of God. The old reality persists; it prowls about like a lion, a wounded lion (I Peter 5:8). But there is also already a new reality hidden beneath the old. "The Christian message," said Paul Tillich, "is the message of a new Reality in which we can participate, and which gives us the power to take anxiety and despair upon ourselves."[8] The important words here are found in the latter phrase: the new Reality *gives us the power to take anxiety and despair upon ourselves*. The gospel does not simply dispel every cause for anxiety and despair, and when it is presented as if it does that, it is reduced to simplistic and sentimental nonsense that only the naive can accept. But the gospel does give us the courage to accept and confront what makes for anxiety and despair. We may choose the new Reality while keeping our eyes wide open with respect to the old. Choose the new! Choose life!

4 When Choice Becomes Necessity

Our hesitation in the face of this commandment is also alleviated considerably today by the very starkness of the realities confronting us. It is almost literally a case of life or death. The decision to choose life becomes less frightening, somehow, once you have caught a glimpse of the contemporary *alternatives* to the choice of life. Those for instance who have looked even a little way into the future hell of a nuclear holocaust, as has Dr. Helen Caldicott,* are apt to think that the choice of life in the face of such a war is not just a possibility but a veritable necessity. It is as if history itself were (so to speak) pushing us off the end of the diving board into the water. We who have been teetering there so nervously, afraid to choose, afraid to take the plunge into an active participation in life are like the children of Israel at the edge of the Red Sea: the presence of death at our backs greatly encourages us to brave the waves of the sea of life. There are really only the two alternatives after all, as the Deuteronomist has known all along: we shall either have to choose life today, or else we shall have chosen—by thousands of little *in*decisions, likely—we shall have chosen death.

The sheer starkness of the alternatives is new for us North Americans. Heretofore, our modern world view has conditioned us to think that there were before us an infinite variety of choices, and all of them, in the long run, were positive. It was

*A physician, featured in the film "If You Love This Planet," National Film Board of Canada.

not a question of whether we would or would not be great; it was only the choice of how to achieve the greatness that was our manifest destiny. So we New World folk are hardly prepared for the simplicity and the starkness of the choices that Doctor Deuteronomy puts before us, that our own historical moment has put before us. We thought—well, we were constantly assured—that life was inevitable: a more and more and more abundant life! The advertisers are still trying to sing that song, but it has become a little silly. (Is this why so many of the TV ads come off a species of slapstick humor?) Those who have taken something like honest stock of our situation know that we are being brought back to this old, biblical reality: that there are finally only two choices. Life and good, death and evil. Naturally that jars us! To take it in, we have to subject our intellects and spirits to a whole new set of assumptions. We have to unlearn the religion of progress. And that is hard.

But (says our biblical mentor) it is not too hard. It is not "across the sea" (verse 13) . . . It is not only over there in old Europe, where people never lost sight of death and the tragic, even when they entered the modern era. It is not only in the wisdom of our parental culture that we can look for help in making this transition to the life-and-death situation into which time has ushered us. Our own pioneers, and the people who were here to meet them: *they* understood something of this deuteronomical logic. Our first parents on this continent were poor people. They were indeed the Third World people of their time: poor, marginalized, confronted by the harsh realities of an Old World society that held only death for them. They chose life, though it was by no means easy. It never is. Their choice of life meant in fact, as we know, that they had to assume risks and hardships and crushing loneliness and other problems of the kind they'd never have tasted if they had decided to stay at home and die quietly of starvation and hopelessness in their European beds, or in the street of those newly industrialized towns to which they flocked in droves in the vain hope of employment. When we tell our story, we North Americans, we too often forget these beginnings, overly impressed as we all too soon became with the so-called success that came later on. If we could get back behind the glitter of Enlightenment rhetoric that has dictated much too long the tone of our text books and our self-images, we might find resources of courage for making the choice for life that has again in our time been put to us by divine Providence. Why should we assume that we have only one song to sing? Why should we behave as if we were locked into a religion of unending technical progress, ever-expanding economic growth, and therefore (given the international situation) an economy of war? Why should *this* mindset so dominate our spirits? There was once another, humbler vision taking shape on these shores. Oh, certainly it was never pure. There is no need to be romantic about our beginnings. But I suspect that the humbler vision had more promise of life in it than the grand enterprise that the 18th and 19th centuries dubbed "the American Dream." There is, you see, a precedent for the choice of life, life as distinct from our way of life, here in our own history. And there are minorities in our midst, too, who can teach us the difference between choosing real life and simply opting for more of what we already have.

The commandment within the gospel of life does not lie over the sea, then. We need not excuse ourselves on the basis of our innocency, our lack of the experience of alternative styles of life. There are alternatives in our past and in our midst. The commandment to choose life speaks to us out of our own environment. It is there in the everyday realities that form our home, in the trees that we pass on our way to work, trees that are dying from (among other things) the exhaust fumes of the cars in which we enclose ourselves while passing the trees. It has to do with the things we say to our children, the values we silently enshrine in our houses, the way we spend our money, the manner in which we conceive of Russians and Blacks and Whites and Women and Men and Children. You do not have to go far afield to find out the implications of this law within the gospel. It is right here in the polling booths from which Americans and Canadians stay away in droves, in the stores where we spend our money and in the churches where (probably) we keep most of it in our wallets. We are not being asked to change the world *all by ourselves,* without any precedent, without any experience. We are simply being asked to participate in the change that the Holy Spirit, "the Lord and Giver of Life," is bringing to pass in a world where change has become a matter of necessity.

5 "Jesus Christ, the Life of the World"

I have been reflecting upon the mandate of our mission, that is, the command we are given as those who have heard the gospel of God's new covenant with life. But someone will want to know, What has this to do with proclaiming the name and power of Jesus Christ and seeking to convert persons and nations to him? Isn't this just a humanistic misinterpretation of the gospel, turning the message of the Bible into life-affirmation?

I know that this question is present everywhere in the churches today. No sooner have concerned Christians begun to think and behave as if, in such a world as ours, the gospel would have to mean confessing that Jesus Christ is indeed the *life* of the world, the life *of the world*, and no sooner have significant minorities in all of our denominations made this discovery, than others, styling themselves Defenders of the True Faith, have accused these minorities of selling out to "humanism" and, in some cases, "Communism" and the like. It is one of the most pathetic aspects of ecclesiastical life today that so many good, thinking people in the churches are unnerved by the accusations and innuendos of the "true believers" that they must expend a great deal of energy placating this so-called conservative element. I am acquainted with a good many leaders in the ecumenical church who seem almost afraid to be *too* life-affirming in case they are perceived by true believers as having exchanged the Christian faith for a slightly-disguised ethical humanism.

It is time therefore for those who believe that Jesus Christ is the life *of the world* to assume the offensive and to put certain very serious theological questions to those who feel themselves the guardians of orthodoxy, and make the mission of the Church a blatant bid for converts to their doctrines. We who are reared in the traditions of liberal fair-mindedness and live-and-let-live have, it seems to me, been much too tolerant of the captivity of the Christian faith on this continent by its most simplistic, one-sided and doctrinaire forms. Ernst Kasemann in his *Jesus Means Freedom*[9] and elsewhere asked the self-proclaimed Christian conservatives some embarrassing questions. But Kasemann's approach has been the exception rather than the rule with Christian scholars. Most of the intellectual Christians that I know have never read a word by Hal Lindsey, and many of them do not know who he is. Not even his name! The great majority of professional theologians, in my experience, never look at television religion despite the known fact that this, and not what they offer in their writings and their classrooms, is what has become *normative Christianity* on this continent. It seems to me high time that serious Christianity took some initiative in this matter.

Over and against the interpretation of the gospel as God's covenant with life, the so-called evangelicals insist that our mission is to persuade people to "accept Jesus Christ as Lord and Saviour." But I should like to know: What exactly does this mean? What does such a formula stand for? Having an ecstatic spiritual experience? Assenting to certain carefully selected biblical affirmations, most of them lifted out of their contexts, both their scriptural contexts and their historical contexts? Mouthing predictable religious language in prayer and greeting, passwords (as it were) that enable like-minded believers to recognize you as one of themselves and not one of the sinners and tax collectors? What does it all mean? What in the world does it come to? What does it come to *in the world?*

On the whole, it seems to come to a religious brand of garden-variety self-satisfaction: a sort of stained-glass version of middle-class euphoria, a high that can be enjoyed in private but mostly in gangs and is displayed as a spectator sport on television. Objectively speaking, this grand program of getting people to say that they love Jesus appears to have the end effect of removing from the world Jesus loved a great many human beings who might otherwise have exercised some genuine responsibility for its future. If this is really the mission of the Christian Church, then it is not surprising that so many of the people in our world who, in the tradition of Jesus, are really sacrificing their personal lives for the life of the world do not find the Christian faith a sufficiently generous credo for their vocation. They are not interested in a religion that thinks that it has scored points for God when it has caused Jews and humanists and Marxists and atheists and former Presbyterians to say "Jesus loves *me*" and then proceed, as "born-again Christians," to manifest singular unconcern for the planet and its suffering.

Those who are really giving their lives for the world's life today are too altruistic to be concerned primarily for their own personal salvation, and they are likely, these contemporary "children of peace," to find the building of crystal cathedrals rather obscene.

Must we not have done with this blasphemy of a world-conquering—that is, a world-negating—"mission" in the name of Jesus? Should we not rather begin to ask seriously about the Jesus who gave his life for the world that God so loved? How did it happen that Jesus, whose whole life was offered in suffering love *for* this world, became the Jesus who has to conquer everything and everybody and get them to say "Lord, Lord, Saviour, Saviour," or consign them to some nuclear hell?

What does *conserving* the gospel mean in such a world as ours? Would it not mean attempting to conserve, indeed to recover, the biblical picture of a crucified One who through taking upon himself the consequences of the world's option for death made a bridgehead in history for life to enter? I am interested in rediscovering the meaning of the mission of *that* Jesus; and I suspect that it doesn't have very much to do with getting people to say "Lord, Lord." And I know that it has nothing at all to do with persuading them that Jesus wants them to be millionaires!

What it does have to do with is participating in Jesus' own mission—the implementation of God's everlasting covenant with life. The mission of the Church is the stewardship of life.

We've been treating stewardship in our churches as a second-rate thing, a means to some other end. The end for us too, not only for the sectarian conservatives, has too often been a slightly more sophisticated version of getting people to say "Lord, Lord." As I read the newer Testament, that was by no means the end that Jesus himself sought. Surely he understood his own work, not at the end but as the means: namely as the means to the end that human beings might love God and one another and their nonhuman counterparts and their unique and beautiful world. In short, the end that they might . . . "choose life": actually choose it, not just be! It seems to me that all the theology, the christology, the theories of the atonement, the services of worship, *all* of these are nothing but the means. The end of the matter is that gratitude for being that issues in thanksgiving and in the nurturing of life in all of its variety and wonder. Our mission *is* the stewarding of life. And of this I am positive: If in this kingdom of death we really are life's stewards; if in the face of our world's covenant with death we are truly faithful to the God who in Jesus Christ made a new covenant with creation, then we shall never lack for opportunities to tell others the reason why. Never!

DIALOGUE

Question: How do you know what visionaries to trust? There are
lots of dreamers around. Some of them are institutionalized! A
great many of the visionaries who are writing and singing and
marching in protests today would be absolute disasters if you
put them into the oval office. Haven't you yourself said that the
basic trouble with this New World of ours is that it was based
on a dream, the American Dream? So can you now tell us that
we need a vision?

Response: Well said! Let me try to state as clearly as I can what
for me would constitute an *authentic* vision, i.e., what would be
the test of good social dreaming. It would be this: Has this 'visionary' ever really experienced the night? I mean, how deep is
his/her exposure to the awesome and negating things that happen to people in this world? To use the metaphor I've been
employing throughout these meditations: Does this person who
wants to lead us into life know anything, really, about death?

Martin Luther King would pass such a test, in my judgment,
because his famous dream of justice and equality for Blacks
grew out of a deep and informed involvement with the life of
the Black community in the U.S.A. So do I trust dreamers like
Elie Wiesel and Hannah Arendt and many other Jewish people
of our time, because those visions were made in Auschwitz, or
its terrible light. The Ehrlichs, whom I quoted in this meditation,
are scientists who have explored in depth and with great intellectual courage many of the very negating things that are going
on in the world of nature on account of our human behavior and
priorities. So when they conclude their book with a plea for their
readers to become visionaries, they aren't just mouthing sentimental platitudes.

In other words, a price has to be paid for great visions, and
the price is always some form of personal suffering. Christians
ought not to find that surprising, since at the core of our belief
is the story of One who dreamt of a peaceable kingdom from
the vantage point of a cross.

It is in this connection that I would speak to your reference
concerning my criticism of the American Dream. The vision that
was entertained by the first European settlers on this continent

(as well as many who have come to these shores since) was not, in my view, inappropriate or inauthentic. I am referring to the ordinary people, the displaced persons, the Third World of their time, who looked for a place to pursue their modest hopes. They *had* paid the price for those hopes: they were not cheap hopes! These persons had been pushed out of their Old World, and they could only inherit this new home through much travail. It was only when this modest vision of theirs was taken into (co-opted by) the Great Success Story that became the American Dream that something went wrong with it. It became too grandiose, too propagandistic, because it no longer emanated from the souls of those who knew oppression, but was transformed into the triumph song of history's winners. So, not surprisingly, it became in turn an ideological tool of oppression. To use some of the terminology I have already explained in these sessions, the thing that began as a modest vision of new beginnings became, during the 18th and 19th centuries particularly, the ideology of the successful and thus, ironically, the rhetoric by which they justified their right to continue living successfully in spite of what that meant for other peoples, including some within their own midst.

So I am not against dreams! "Without a vision, the people perish." But history teaches us how yesterday's dreams can so easily become today's propaganda. This means there must always be a critical *rethinking* of dreams in the light of their actual function. Do they serve the life of some while causing the death of others? What constitutes this life that they promise? Do they help us to be truthful about the world, or do they put blinkers on us so that we only see what they intend us to see? Having begun in some night, are these dreams now parading about as if they were the only Light of the World—or are they still struggling with new and ever subtler forms of darkness?

Question: You've said that we should treat creation as a gift so precious that we are willing to make personal sacrifices so that it can be enjoyed by generations to come. Personally, I like that. I'm sick to heart over the political cynicism that thinks ahead only so far as the next election. But what can you do? With an economic system that assumes as its basic presupposition that everybody should plunder the natural world as much as possible, that the whole human community will be better off eventually if individuals work with might and main to make themselves a million, doesn't all talk of restraint and sacrifice sound like so much froth?

Response: Yes. And so the answer is: *Get a better economic system!* Capitalism is an 18th century vision that does not, in my opinion, meet the test I have just said should be applied to social visions. It never did! It was hatched, this particular dream, in the studies of privileged persons who had little or no knowledge of the grovelling poverty that was already eating away at the globe's population. (Or, if they had such knowledge, they cynically regarded free enterprise as a way of solving the population problem.) They were, moreover, individuals who, because they were so insulated from life's negating dimensions on a societal scale, were able to interpret the Christian religion in terms of a view of Providence that was theoretical indeed: an invisible hand would arrange all our selfish economic pursuits so as to benefit the totality. It is still possible to hear this fatuous product of 18th century deism and middle-class ambition proclaimed from high places. Today, when the media bring starving citizens of Ethiopia and Chad and oppressed peoples of Latin America right into one's living room, it is an even more irresponsible "vision" than it was two centuries ago.

Let me insert here at once: Those who hear this kind of criticism of capitalism as if it were the product of *Communist* dreaming are simply skirting the issue. There are *inherent* flaws in capitalism itself, and treating all criticisms of capitalism as if they cloaked a Communist plot is simply a way of avoiding these flaws. My criticism of the capitalist system is a consequence of my Christian belief. I can't think how *Christians* could ever have endorsed an economic system that raises egotism to a virtue and the acquisition of money, property and power to a divine mandate. And where in the Scriptures do we hear that divine Providence achieves this fantastic redistribution of things so sweetly that everybody benefits from the selfishness of those who are best at accumulating things and raping the earth? What I read in the Bible is that the earth "and the fulness thereof" belongs to the Lord.

To be critical of capitalism does not mean to attack democracy. There are clear lines of continuity between democracy and the Christian understanding of human nature and human community. But democracy is not to be equated with economic capitalism, and in fact there are aspects of the democratic ideal, such as equal opportunity, that are almost totally destroyed by unchecked capitalism.

It seems to me crystal clear that if the spirit of capitalism continues to dominate in First World societies, our planet is doomed. Fortunately, this spirit has already been checked in many First World societies, and the mounting crises of the economy, of resources, of the environment, and of population necessitate its serious revision everywhere. Christians are in a position to influence this revision, because we have a unique understanding of the delicate balance and tension between the individual and the community, an understanding that is neither capitalistic nor Communistic. But if we are to exercise such influence, more of us will have to stop behaving as if capitalism were our own *legitimate* child and recognize the theological and ethical blunders that allowed it to come to birth in our midst.

Question: When you say that death is a great power in our world, aren't you giving death too much credit? As Christians we believe in the victory of the resurrection. Death has "lost its sting." Aren't you taking death too seriously?

Response: It's funny. Some people think what I am saying in these meditations is too visionary, utopian, unrealistic, and so forth. Others, like yourself apparently, want me to become still more optimistic. On the whole, I find it a good sign that this is so, because I don't think Christian faith should be equated with either pessimism or optimism. I always expect the pessimists to find what I am saying too positive, and the optimists to find it too negative. It's sort of a test of authentic theology for me.

Against the people who want to be realistic to the point of vowing that nothing can be altered, faith says: There is a grace abroad in the world that introduces new possibilities . . . even at the edge of the Red Sea. And against the people who want to believe that *everything* is possible, faith says: Keep your eyes open and don't give in to the urge to cheer prematurely.

Technically speaking, it's a question of one's *eschatology.* There have always been Christians who believed that all the good things lay in the future, and therefore didn't expect much from this life. And there have been others who claimed that the kingdom of God is already here, or just around the corner. Personally, I want to say both—"already" and "not yet." Already we are forgiven, but we are not yet sinless. Already we can begin to love one another, but there is still plenty of alienation and resentment among us. Let's face it! Already we are "members one of another," but we are not yet fully "at one." Already there are possibilities for change and reshaping the world, because God is making all things new. But we are not yet the new Jerusalem. Already (yes, all right) death has lost its sting, but it is still "the last enemy," still to be decisively done in.

The danger of every eschatology that overlooks the already is that it tends to satisfy itself with the status quo. The danger of eschatologies that overlook the not yet is, however, just as grave, because they tend to ignore the real evil that continues to exist in the world in order to maintain intact their spiritual sense of completion and well-being.

So in the end, both the realized (already) and futuristic (not yet) eschatologies produce an ethic that leaves the world as it is. The one because it thinks the world can't be changed. The other because it refuses to take seriously what needs changing.

When you live *between* the already and the not yet of Christ's victory, you are more likely to develop *an ethic of worldly hope.* This ethic is honest about what is wrong in the world because it knows that the world's salvation is *not yet* finished. It is at the same time, however, orientated towards changing what is wrong with the world because it believes that God is *already* transforming it in ways that are both mysterious and ordinary.

Question: I take it that you find a real distinction between the way we started out as a people here in North America and what became of us under the impact of the Enlightenment and the Industrial and technological revolutions. I think that makes some sense. But haven't we perhaps gone so far in the direction of the success myth that it's hard for us to get back to that humbler vision?

Response: I agree that it is very hard for us to recover our own modest beginnings. Part of the reason is that we've incorporated exactly those modest beginnings *into* our success story. The first part of the story (Act I, so to speak) likes to have us the underdogs of the world so that our eventual success can seem all the more phenomenal. Horatio Alger! Our most characteristic folk heroes are little guys who made it big. They showed 'em!

But what if you want to say that it was better before we got big? That our beginnings weren't just beginnings, the prelude to the real thing, but contained better goals and values than the ones we have ended up with? All over the world people look at the TV serial, "Dallas," and think: "That's America!" And many of *us* think so too. But is *that* what the Pilgrim fathers and mothers were really after? Is downtown Toronto, with its much advertised "CN Tower" what my poor Irish and North-of-England ancestors came to this continent to erect? I doubt it. "Dallas" is nothing but the story of a society in decay. And so what if you can build a city "with its tower reaching into the heavens," a communications tower no less, if you have nothing wise or beautiful to communicate, if at the base of that same tower you find racial alienation and porn shops?

In some ways our continental story really does parallel the biblical story, though not in the ways we usually think. Israel too made it into a land flowing with milk and honey, and proceeded to forget the hope to which it was being called in its wanderings. The prophets were always trying to recall those modest beginnings, not because they liked being homeless and poor, but because the children of Israel were more genuine then; they lost something vital to their rudimentary vision when they settled down. Similarly, the Church is called to be a *communio viatorum*, "a people of the way." Not a people that has arrived. Arriving, settling down, becoming "successful," the Bible worries a good deal about that. The reason, I think, is that its writers know on the one hand that success of that sort is an illusion, and on the other that we human beings really are at our best when we're . . . trail-blazing.

It's true, the earlier vision is hard to remember. But it is not impossible. And Christians have the advantage of this sort of biblical logic, a kind of road map "on the Way."

FIFTH MEDITATION

THE GOAL OF OUR MISSION: ABUNDANT LIFE

". . . behold, I create new heavens
and a new earth;
and the former things shall not be remembered
or come into mind.
But be glad and rejoice for ever
in that which I create;
for behold, I create Jerusalem a rejoicing,
and her people a joy.
I will rejoice in Jerusalem
and be glad in my people;
no more shall be heard in it the sound of weeping
and the cry of distress,
No more shall there be in it
an infant that lives but a few days,
or an old man who does not fill out his days,
for the child shall die a hundred years old,
and the sinner a hundred years old shall be
accursed.
They shall build houses and inhabit them;
they shall plant vineyards and eat their fruit.
They shall not build and another inhabit;
they shall not plant and another eat;
for like the days of a tree shall the days of my people
be,
and my chosen shall long enjoy the work of
their hands,
They shall not labor in vain,
or bear children for calamity;
for they shall be the offspring of the blessed of the
Lord,
and their children with them.
Before they call I will answer,
while they are still speaking I will hear.
The wolf and the lamb shall feed together,
the lion shall eat straw like the ox;
and dust shall be the serpent's food.
They shall not hurt or destroy in all my holy mountain,
says the Lord."
—Isaiah 65:17–25

1 The Spiritualization of the Christian Message

When in that unforgettable line of the tenth chapter of his Gospel the one identified as John has our Lord say to his listeners that he came "that they might have life, and have it more abundantly," I wonder if he did not have in mind such a passage of the Hebraic Scriptures as this. It may be a testimony to the authenticity of these words of Jesus that they are retained in that account of his life and teaching that scholars suppose to have been most strongly influenced by Hellenistic traditions. As a Jew, Jesus of Nazareth naturally would have thought of abundance of life in terms of the concerns that inform Isaiah's vision of God's redemptive work: human joy; the end of weeping and suffering; the end too of being shunted about from place to place, never able to enjoy the house one built or the field one broke; longevity, health, and meaningful work; justice; a sense of the immediacy of God's presence, answering prayer before it is finished; harmony among all the diverse creatures—the peaceable kingdom; and no more violence: "They shall not hurt or destroy in all my holy mountain." This is no pie-in-the-sky-by-and-by. It's a very earthy vision; and many things in the newer Testament, even in that much-maligned and misunderstood Apocalypse of John, are reminiscent of just this earthy dimension of the tradition of Jerusalem. Clearly this is the matrix out of which sprang that *communio viatorum*, that people of the way, which was the earliest Christian movement.

But very soon in its history there were influences upon that way that distanced it from these original roots in the faith of Israel. In some ways it was a miracle that the divorce from Israel was not more conclusive than it was. At moments in the history of the early church, large segments of the church were clearly tempted to drop the Jewish connection altogether. Under the impact of gnosticism, mystery cults, and other powerful trends within the Hellenistic world, the church very nearly capitulated to the temptation to disassociate itself entirely from the religion of the older Testament. It proved to be too difficult to bring this off entirely, because of course the church remembered that Jesus himself was a Jew, and that his teaching had depended largely upon Jewish prophetic faith, wisdom literature, and history. Moreover, the early church (Paul particularly) had seen what occurred with and to Jesus as a *culmination* of the promises made to Israel. So that in the long run Christianity retained the Jewish connection in spite of its obvious temptation to drop it and strike out as an entirely independent religion.

While the formal continuity with Israel was retained, however, many of the emphases that are present in the faith of Israel and expressed in the older Testament were lost or significantly altered through reinterpretation. Christianity did not become just another of the many religions of the Hellenistic world. Created by the military exploits of Alexander the Great, that world was a mishmash of human cultures and cults incorporating Egyptian, Persian, Greek and many other elements. Christianity managed to keep a little distance from that eclectic world, but it tended rather soon in its life to take on one of the primary features of that Hellenistic world view, namely, the tendency to renounce this world, to despise the flesh, to locate the principle of evil in matter, and so to seek redemption in the beyond. The tendency, in other words, to spiritualize the message of and about Jesus as the Christ.

There were, of course, also Jewish sects that were influenced by Hellenistic religious patterns. It would have been impossible to live in that cultural atmosphere without being swept along by some of its assumptions. But the main stream of Judaism managed, it seems to me, to escape the permanent imprinting of its faith by Hellenistic spiritualism in a way that Christianity did not. Even to this day, Judaism can read a passage like Isaiah 65 and not immediately allegorize it, or turn it into otherworldly longing, the beautiful isle of somewhere. Without condoning everything that emanates from the modern state of Israel, we must surely recognize in the vision that created and sustains it a firm continuity with the prophets' insistence that the redeeming God has precisely *this* world in mind as the site of God's 'new creation.'

For redemption in the tradition of Jerusalem is a this-worldly category. Unlike Hellenistic religion, the religion of the Jews was and is grounded in the belief that this world, being the creation of the good God, is itself *in essence* (that is, in terms of God's intention for it and in terms of its basic potentiality) *good.* We hardly need to add that Israel neither was, nor is, naive about evil, sin, suffering, death—all the negating things that are actually present in the Jerusalem tradition. It is hard to find in the annals of history, analyses of evil more subtle and more convincing than that which informs the whole Hebraic Bible from Genesis III onwards.

Israel takes evil with great seriousness precisely *because* it also knows about the potential for good within the historical condition. But it does not equate evil *with* the historical condition, with matter, with time, with the flesh. Evil is a spiritual reality and it is inseparable from the same human spirituality that is the locus of our potential for goodness. Thus it would have been (and is) impossible, unthinkable, for such a faith to regard *salvation* as an ultimate separation of spirit from matter. What we need to be saved from is not the world of flesh and blood and bone and gland, but from our own distorted *spiritual* misuse of life. Thus whenever Israel rehearsed its story of salvation and its hope for ultimate salvation, as in this passage from Isaiah, it pictured a renewal of creation *through* the renewal, the cleansing, the judging of our human attitudes towards creation: "Create *in me* a clean heart, O God, and renew a right spirit with *me.*" "I will write my law *on their hearts!*" It is not creation that is to be cast aside by the God who liberates his people from their oppression, but it is our prideful, slothful mentality with respect to our own creatureliness. The object of redemption is not that we should be rescued *from* the world, but that we should be rescued *for* it. For life!

Christianity, or at least a very significant dimension of the Christian faith, took another turn. The earliest Christians, inspired by *some* of the things they might have heard from Jesus, or thought they heard, but hearing these things now in the enticing sociological context of an apocalyptic age and an otherworldly religious atmosphere, began to manifest a special interest in eternity, an eternity that no longer conditioned and altered the quality of time; an eternity that beckoned one beyond time, beyond this vale of tears. This world would in any case, they believed, soon come to an end. Jesus would return, judge the earth, and establish his heavenly kingdom. When that did not happen, the spiritualistic interpretation of the gospel continued to be dominant, but now in a more personalistic way: When you die you will go to be with Jesus in paradise, where (as he said) he is already preparing a place for you. And some added: If you die a martyr to the Christian cause you will have a special place in heaven. That teaching so caught on that finally warnings had to be issued to Christians not to *seek* martyrdom.

Now there were certain dimensions of the Christian teaching that could foster this kind of spiritualization of the gospel. Perhaps some of them are from Jesus himself. But in my opinion these aspects of the faith would not have become dominant had it not been for the fact that in the context of that very apocalyptic age many people had already given up on the world, and were ready to follow any imaginative religion that could offer them a spiritual escape from the harsh realities of everyday life. For the poorer elements of that society, life was indeed harsh— hard and brutish and short! There was no such thing as upward mobility, the improvement of one's lot through industry, intelligence, initiative. Was one born a slave? Then one would remain a slave. And remember: most of those from whom the early church drew its membership belonged to these lower strata of society, including the slaves. One cannot blame them for finding in Christianity, as they found in other religions and quasi-religions of their world, hope for fulness of life in an afterworld that would perhaps make up for the brutality and suffering of this one.

All the same, something happened to Christianity in this period of the first three or four centuries. Not only did it cut itself loose from its moorings in Hebraic religion, but it became increasingly otherworldly. The life it offered people was a life beyond this world; and consequently it tended to denigrate this world, to shun and ridicule its paltry promises and delights, to cultivate a special consciousness of its moral wickedness, to offer heaven as a solace for earth. "Earth hath no sorrows that heaven cannot heal." We have never overcome this influence!

It may be humanly understandable: there is much in this world, in the creaturely condition itself, with its vulnerability and its complex patterns of evil and suffering, that often causes the human soul to long for . . . heavenly rest. But in the process of turning away from this world Christianity lost something that is surely of its essence: namely, the rootedness of the divine love in history. A faith that not only follows in the path of the prophets of Israel, but has at its center the announcement of God's Word made flesh, and in the flesh suffering and dying for the world's salvation: such a faith can hardly turn itself towards the skies without turning away from something vital to its own rudimentary message. As the great Roman Catholic theologian, Karl Rahner, wrote in his book, *Mission and Grace:*[1]

> In the Incarnation and the Cross God has made a total and final decision (without prejudice to human freedom) in favor of the world and the natural order as saved, glorified and to be given beatitude through the victory of grace. The drama is no longer in the balance; world history is already, in principle, decided, and the decision is for its salvation. But given that this unity of the created and redemptive orders has already entered upon the eschatological stage . . . it is then inadmissible for a Christian, faced with the task of believing in this fact (improbable as it is, and seemingly contradicted at every turn by secular experience), to conduct his life, in the concrete, as though this unity were still historically in the balance. *Post Christum natum* he simply must be more hopeful in his thinking about the world than he need have been (or could have been) before he knew that the Word of God has taken to himself forever the flesh of this world.

The question that confronts us today is how we can recover something of this earthward orientation of the gospel of incarnation and cross. Or, to put it in the terms of the chief metaphor of our present reflections: How can we describe the life of which we are made stewards in *this*-worldly terms and still remain faithful to the *core* of the Christian tradition? I want to return to that question later.

2 The Other Side of the Coin: Christian Worldliness

But before I do so it is necessary to consider another side of the fate of Christianity in its early formation. We have seen that influential segments of the early church introduced a process of the spiritualization of the Christian message, ending with a gospel that saved people from the life of the world rather than for it. But perhaps you have noticed that whenever there is an overemphasis upon things spiritual and a noncommitant putdown of the physical, there is usually a reaction from the latter side. Even before the fourth century, there were people who complained about the tendency of some of the Christians to become so spiritualistic that they neglected their responsibilities for and in the material world, including their responsibilities for the poorer members of their own *koinonia*. But in the fourth century, something happened that brought about this other, material side of human nature forcibly: the Emperor Constantine, who seems not to have been a very bright individual but who certainly possessed considerable political savvy, saw that the Christian church could be a beneficial spiritual force for pulling together his divided and disintegrating empire; and, as we have seen, by the end of that same century one of Constantine's successors, Theodosius, had outlawed every other religion except Christianity—Christianity as practiced by the court. Christendom had begun! What had started as a small, illicit movement within Judaism, but increasingly outside of it, now set out on a journey to become a great institution, with growing political power and worldly glory.

What we have then (what we still have, in a great variety of forms) are essentially two types of Christianity: the one spiritualistic and otherworldly (frequently anti-worldly), the other materialistic and worldly. The one offering fulness of life on the other side of the grave, the other prospering on this side of the grave, calling that prosperity "life," and claiming it, in fact, as an advance installment of divine approval. The one type answering the question about the meaning of life by saying that life is what God is going to give us when we have finally sloughed off this mortal coil, when we have been freed by death from the plaguing drives of hunger and sex and the need for shelter and security; the other type answering the question about the meaning of life by saying that God is certainly going to give us fulness of life right now, if we are good, and reward us already by making us successful and rich and content.

I am of course not claiming that there are no alternatives to these two types of Christianity. I mean only that they have been powerful throughout subsequent history; and we can still find them today, vying with one another for our attention and our

souls, sometimes offered by one and the same evangelistic community in strange and inconsistent admixtures of messages. On
the one hand we are told that as Christians we should turn away
from every worldly pleasure, despise this world's goods, keep
our body and its passions and lusts under constant surveillance.
On the other hand we are promised that if we are really among
the elect, God is going to reward us here and now with very tangible rewards: "Jesus wants you to be a millionaire!"

Is either of these forms of the Christian faith authentic in relation to our scriptural roots? Clearly, both of them can find, here
and there, texts and scraps of biblical ideas to support them.
What can one not find in the Bible if one is looking for it hard
enough? The long Christian *tradition* offers even more variety.
But are these answers to the question, What is life? What is the
"abundant life" that is the goal of our mission, the basic two
alternatives from which we must choose?

It is my opinion that they are not. I want to reject on one hand
the spiritualistic answer that finds life over there, because it
seems to me that our faith does have something vital to do with
this life, this here and now. On the other hand, I am by no means
content with the materialistic answer that finds life's meaning
bound up with things and success and money and fame and
power. What answer can we discover to this knotty question that
avoids both the otherworldliness of the first answer and the
sheer, uncritical this-worldliness of the second?

Let us listen again to our teacher, Isaiah:
*" . . . I create new heavens and a new earth . . . be glad and re-
joice in that which I create; . . . no more shall be heard . . . the
sound of weeping and the cry of distress. No more shall there
be . . . an infant that lives but a few days, or an old man who does
not fill out his days . . . They shall build houses and inhabit them;
they shall plant vineyards and eat their fruit. . . . They shall not
labor in vain, or bear children for calamity . . . Before they call
I will answer . . . The wolf and the lamb shall feed
together . . . They shall not hurt or destroy in all my holy
mountain,*
                                        says the Lord."

3 Life as Process and as Vision

The first thing one notices about this statement (and we know
it is typical of many statements in both the older and the newer
testaments) is that it has a future thrust. It is a *vision* of what
could be—no, of what is truly coming to be; for its presupposition is faith in the Lord who speaks, and whose speech is not
in vain but creates (if need be from nothing) what it promises:

"I am making a new earth . . . " The fulness of life is . . . not yet; but it is underway, it is coming to pass.

How important visions are to human existence! In the previous Dialogue, I referred to Martin Luther King's famous speech, "I have a dream. . . ." "Without a vision, the people perish" (Proverbs 29:18). In my Third Meditation, I said that part of the trouble with our old mainline churches is that we lack vision. Visions are born in the night, as the prophet Daniel said, and we are mostly afraid to go far enough into our night, into the real darkness of contemporary life, to put ourselves in the way of having any gripping visions of what might be, of what shall be! But our hesitancy is the source of a vicious circle, because it is only from our visions that we human beings derive the courage to go on, and until we risk the darkness long enough to see great visions again, our churches, I think, will be confined to the sort of half-life that is the lot of those who dwell in the twilight zone, the neither hot nor cold, to use another metaphor that the church had to have applied to it early in its life (Rev. 3:15). There is of course a good deal of loose talk in churches, as in our society at large, about visions. Every new Christian education wing is launched with the rhetoric of the new vision, just as at the secular level the politicians announce their scarcely distinguishable political alternatives as containing new visions. But visions are not so readily come by. The prophets had to suffer for their visions. Think of Jeremiah! Amos! Think of Jesus! Think too of the great artists, musicians, explorers of the dark secrets of nature. It is not, I believe, that suffering is in some simple way the condition for greatness. That's a rather romantic myth entertained mostly by people who do not suffer very much. Suffering as such does not produce greatness either of art or life. But without some deep personal exposure to that which negates, positive accounts of the world tend to be superficial. They falsify existence because they know nothing of the violence that is the other side of peace, the grasping that is the other side of justice, the hate that is the other side of love, the despair that is the other side of hope. Knowledge of the world's darkness is the precondition for accounts of light. As Hans Kung has put it, "Coping with the negative side of life is the acid test of Christian and non-Christian humanisms."[2] Sometimes I tell my students: When you take stock of your Christian faith and your theology, then always ask yourself, 'What must I leave out of account in order to believe this that I believe?' The answer, I tell them, must be: 'Nothing!'

What I mean is that visions (for theology too, if it's worth its salt, is a vision) are not to be trusted unless they emerge out of a struggle with all that would cancel the visionary aspect of one's account of reality. Martin Luther's vision was and is credible because with every line, every sentence of it I know that I am reading the tortured confession of hope of a man who knew the meaning of despair. Martin Luther King's dream was credible too. A great many Black people in the U.S.A. believed it and still do: because it was born in their night, the night they know and have known. Women today, many of them, and not only in the field of Christian thought, are saying and writing and doing things that many other women (and men) can understand, believe, and rejoice in. And why? Because their words and deeds emerge out of a long, silent struggle with that which negates life and cramps the human spirit. Great visions are "born in the night" (as Elie Wiesel said), because it is only as we human beings are brought face-to-face with the truth of our condition, the whole truth, that we can imagine in a way that is both realistic and somehow realizable alternatives to the status quo.

Thus in the midst of oppression, exile, and defeat, the prophets of Israel always reminded the people of their foundational vision, that vision that took shape in the homeless wanderings of Father Abraham and Mother Sarah, in the slave house of Egypt, in the wilderness. Out of their continually renewed knowledge of the night, Israel learned how to speak convincingly of the day. Out of their exposure to oppressive conditions, over and over again, Israel discovered how to envisage the liberty of the children of God. Out of their encounter with death, out of generations upon generations of death, Israel fashioned a believable vision of abundant life. That life was always a matter of . . . resurrection from the dead. From the deadness of despair hope arose, and from the deadness of guilt forgiveness arose, and from the deadness of slavery freedom arose, and from the deadness of defeat courage arose. And what happened that first Easter Sunday is in strict continuity with that thousands-of-years-old experience of resurrection from the dead.

And if I am to answer the question, what is life? What is this "abundant life" that is the goal of our mission?—then I would reply, over against the materialists to begin with, that it is in at least one important dimension a matter of vision. It is the courage to envisage the coming to pass of things that are not now present. It is the courage that is given to those who sit in darkness and the shadow of death to believe that darkness and death are not the goal. It is the refusal to believe that injustice and war and sickness and death are simply inevitable. It is that divine discontent that in the face of "September 1st, 1939" insists with W.H. Auden that we who are certainly comprised of dust are also comprised of eros, of an unquenchable longing for life that rebels against everything that stands in its way. Life is the insatiable sense that we were intended for an abundance of *being* that is not to be confused with an abundance of *hav-*

ing. In our senseless accumulation of this world's goods we try, in vain, to compensate for the being that we lack; but none of the treasures we lay up on earth can secure for us that . . . eternal life. Life as vision is life in a condition of dissatisfaction with the present, a thrusting forward, an expectance like the expectancy of children on Christmas eve. This is where there is more than a merely coincidental concurrence between the biblical concept of hope and the scientific idea of evolution. Loren Eiseley expressed the evolutionary idea in much the same way as I should want to speak of Christian hope:

> "Great Minds have always seen it. That is why man has survived his journey this long. When we fail to wish any longer to be otherwise than what we are, we will have ceased to evolve. Evolution has to be lived forward. I say this as one who has stood above the bones of much that has vanished, and at midnight has examined his own face."[3]

Where there is *life*, there is *hope*. To have ceased hoping is to have ceased living, and *especially* if the reason one has stopped hoping is because one thinks one has arrived!

To illustrate: Recently in my country a very modest, middle-aged, lower-middle-class couple, childless, won some 13 millions of dollars in a lottery. I watched them on television as they were interviewed afterwards. They were simple but very likeable people, a little broken by life I thought. I suspect from their faces that they had hoped for a child, or children. Now they had a great fortune. They spoke hesitantly about what they were going to do with it. Well, they had of course bought a new car. Had their dreams been fulfilled? I wonder. I often think about them. I would conjecture that after a while they will discover, if they haven't done so already, that money, things, material goods are no real answer to their dream of the good life. Looking at them, I had the impression that they already found that out. The woman related how, when she had watched on television as the numbers were drawn, she found herself automatically saying, "No, I hope it isn't our number." When it was their number, she went into the kitchen and sat quietly at the table where her husband was working at something and said, "We've won." And she began to cry . . .

Our hopes are far more mysterious than the kind of optimism that can be satisfied with dollars. Hope is of the essence of our life. In a way it is not there to be satisfied, but to keep us looking forward to . . . tomorrow. That's life. *C'est la vie!*

> 'Hope' is the thing with feathers—
> That perches in the soul—
> And sings the tune without the words—
> And never stops—at all—

> —*Emily Dickinson*

4 Life as a Revolution of Hope

But the other side of this prophetic vision is that it refuses to be merely visionary. It will not permit itself to dissolve into pure spiritualism. Martin Luther King had a dream, yes, but it was not content to wait for the liberation from bondage about which so many of the old spirituals of his race sang, heavenly liberation. The dream looks forward to tomorrow, yes, but not to an indefinite tomorrow, a tomorrow in the sweet by-and-by. It is a vision that has very practical implications for the here and now. It is not the kind of vision behind those religions that Karl Marx rightly said function in the world as opiates to keep us from being dissatisfied with our lot, to keep our attention so fixed on future bliss that we shall be indifferent to the pain of the present. On the contrary, the biblical vision, Isaiah's vision for instance, is a worldly one. It is bent upon expressing itself in deed, here and now. It describes a revolution that is in progress: God's revolution. God is creating everything new. Now! And the new world that God is creating in the midst of the old one has to do with very concrete longings of the human spirit: the longing that babies should live and be healthy, that the infant mortality rate that is so high in the Third World should be altered, drastically. The longing that people should not be pushed about from pillar to post, displaced persons, refugees, but that there should be a place of tranquility for all, a place to call home. The longing that unnecessary disasters should cease, that our children should be spared untimely death and illness, that enmity between the creatures of the earth should give way to harmony among them, that evil should cease. The longing for happy, long and (in the original sense of the word) prosperous lives, lives that can be lived towards and for hope because they are not always being reduced to despair.

Reading Isaiah's vision, who could wonder that the Jews have always, to this day, sought longevity and honored the aged. A story is told among them: There was a pogrom, perhaps it was the great pogrom of 1848. All the Jews of the community were slain, but one remained. He was taken before the Czar himself. "Well," said the ruler of all Russia, "you seem to be a bright enough fellow; and so to show you that we Russians are not an uncivilized people I am going to give you the choice as to how you are to die." "Ah," said the Jew, "I thank you sincerely, majesty, and to show you that I am aware of the highly civilized character of your state, as well as to save you and your people a great deal of trouble, I shall choose . . . old age." ("And, said Robert Lifton, from whom I heard this story, "let us see to it that the world itself dies of old age. It is no doubt a finite planet, but why should we destroy it prematurely?"

We are, you see, far from the spiritualistic answer to the question about the meaning of life, that answer that finds *real* life on the other side, "beyond the beyond." Isaiah evidently believes that this world, for all its pain and ambiguity, has in itself a kind of potentiality for abundance. It can be approximated even now, though it cannot be fully achieved. It is not a matter of our making it happen. Isaiah does not have to be instructed about the limitations of humanity. But God is making it happen, and we are called, invited, to participate in God's work.

I wonder if along the way we Christians did not let go, you know, of something very vital within this tradition of Jerusalem. Isn't it possible that Jesus was more of a Jew than we have given him credit for being? When the disciples of John the Baptist came to Jesus, you remember, and asked if he were the one who was to come, or should they look for another, he pointed to things reminiscent of what Isaiah is speaking about in this Scripture: the sick being healed, the lame walking, the prisoners delivered, the naked clothed, the poor hearing the liberating word of truth. It is not all reserved for the future. It is possible even now. No, it is *not inevitable* (we are now speaking about the modern doctrine of historical progress), but it *is possible.*

And if I am asked, what *is* life according to your tradition, then I should want to answer not only that it is the hope that points us towards tomorrow but the courage to believe that what we hope for is in part already realizable today. It is not necessary that two-thirds of humankind should go to bed hungry every night. It is not necessary that children should die before they have had a chance to live. It is not necessary that old people, alone and bitter in their declining years, should be left in hovels in our cities. There is no law that says that war will always be. Life is not only looking forward to what could be if only . . . Life is also daring to think that what we dream for the earth and for our lives in it could become reality. Not because we are such fantastic beings, capable of anything we set our minds to. No, we are rather mediocre creatures in many ways, without much imagination or courage, and altogether too fixed on comfort to be up to much daring where truth is concerned. But *God* is creating—is daring—a new earth and new heavens. And we are chosen, before we were made we were chosen, to be stewards of God's work in this world. The goal of our mission is nothing more nor less that this: to participate in our Lord's mission to help creation discover and realize the LIFE that is being offered it in the midst of all this death. To help God "change the world," borrowing a phrase from Karl Marx.

Conclusion

Abundant life is the goal of our mission. There are literally no limits to the quality of life that is suggested in that word of Jesus, "abundance." There are quantitative limits placed upon us as human beings and as a species. There are, certainly, limits to growth, limits to accumulation and material achievement, and today the natural world is in a state of rebellion because human beings have not been observing these limits. But there are no limits to the *quality* of life that our Creator-Redeemer God offers us.

There are no limits to love—the love we can show for God, for one another, for the inarticulate creation. We could never exhaust the possibilities of love.

There are no limits to justice—the justice that we can work out for the poor and the oppressed who have been so long with us; justice in relation to the minorities in our own midst; justice in the distribution of earth's treasures that belong, finally, to no one people.

There are no limits to peace—the peace that must address itself to superpowers and minipowers; the peace that will have to be pursued, now, with great patience and understanding until the earth itself has run its course.

These gifts of grace, and all the others that are quite literally too numerous to mention, are inexhaustible and limitless. These resources are infinitely renewable.

In fact, perhaps now we can afford to say this to one another, these gifts of grace can never be fully expressed or contained in the days and moments, the years, the decades of our individual lives; they cannot be used up even by centuries, by millenia. They will still be there when earth itself has grown old and died of old age. No amount of time and space can ever deplete the abundant life that God has to give, and of which God also makes *us* stewards. We Christians know of an immensity of life that always transcends our actual living, that cannot be contained in these old wineskins that are our bodies and spirits. The life that God offers God's creation is immeasurably greater than the creation itself. It is infinite, eternal. It goes on, "world without end." In terms of our personal histories in the world, it will outlast us. It will outlast our world itself. The kingdom of God, which is the biblical symbol for the ongoingness of this new being, this life in abundance, which God has inaugurated, cannot be contained in the old wineskin called Planet Earth any more than it can be housed in our personal "earthen vessels."

It goes on! And nothing, nothing at all, can separate us from it.

But the wonder is that we are permitted to participate in its abundance already, here and now: to share it, to be its stewards. The life for which we long, and for which the whole creation groans, begins already here and now. Let us therefore . . . *choose* life!

DIALOGUE

Question: I find myself agreeing with you about the need to emphasize the this-worldiness of our faith, but at the same time I feel nervous about it. Are we to forget altogether about . . . heaven, or whatever this beyond dimension could be called? Can't we overdo the this-worldiness of the gospel?

Response: Frankly, I doubt it. I suspect that if we really took seriously the beauty and goodness of this world, we would find so much wonder in it and develop so much gratitude for it that we'd uncover, in the process, a new route to that beyond. It would be a route that passes *through* earth, not *by* it, not *over* it, not *around* it. We religious people (not only Christians) have been offering heaven so consistently as an *alternative* to this world that we are blind to the road that leads *from* earth to heaven. To find that road, we have to become more earthy than most of us have dared to be.

In her wonderful book, *The Color Purple*, Alice Walker has one of her characters tell another: "Listen, God loves everything you love—and a mess of stuff you don't. But more than anything else, God love admiration." "You saying God vain?" her companion demands. "Naw, she say. Not vain, just wanting to share a good thing. I think it pisses God off if you walk by the color purple in a field somewhere and don't notice it."[4]

For centuries the church has presented its message largely as a variation on the following theme: If you believe in Jesus and do the right things here on earth, *then you will be rewarded in eternity.* The whole thrust of the thing is in the last clause. What transpires here on earth is at best a prelude to the real thing; more often it's a shabby sort of scene that has to be endured, or a testing-ground full of tricky temptations, or a brief and brutal episode preliminary to peace at the last (if you're good!). The wise will shut their eyes and grit their teeth and rein in their passions and *do good* . . . while there is yet time.

I know that liberal interpretations of Christianity have mitigated this otherworldliness considerably, though not so much as we think. Those of us who are clergy or professional church workers know well enough the experience of finding ourselves saddled with the reputation for keeping people on the straight and narrow, winning souls, being a sky pilot, and the like. Even the most world-orientated of us can't escape the centuries-old image of the priest as one whose basic role is to prepare souls for the life-to-come. I suspect most Christians have a long way to go before they become sufficiently rooted in this world to be perceived as pointers to . . . "the color purple."

What I have been suggesting in these meditations is that we try consciously to reverse this whole process. Instead of presenting eternal life as something that comes afterwards, let us think of it concretely as a quality that belongs to the here-and-now. Instead of reserving all the mystery and beatitude for later, let us regard this globe itself as containing a kind of depth and grandeur that is so astonishing that you can hardly think about it without weeping. We've wasted so much ecstasy on heaven (which doesn't need it) that we white Western peoples have little passion left over for earth. If we have treated the earth in a high-handed fashion, wasting its precious gifts of water and trees and land and all, it is in great measure because we've directed our sense of wonder up there, or, in the later secularized West, in there, i.e., in ourselves. The question that the present manifold crisis of earth puts to us is: Can we think of eternity as a dimension of time and space? Can we feel the Holy unfolding in the everyday? Can we experience grace as something invading every conversation? Can we perceive every tree and bush "aflame with God" (Elizabeth Barrett-Browning)? Can we be in this world witnesses to "the color purple"?

If we can do that, be that sort of people in the world, then heaven will take care of itself. I mean, if people begin to get the notion that earth itself is a place of the most astonishing mystery and beauty, they might be led to conclude that perhaps it really does . . . *go on.*

Question: You said, if I heard you correctly, that one can find anything one wants to find in the Bible. Is that really so?

Response: No. Not *really* so. If one is serious about being a student of the Scriptures, one will discover that there are some things you can't derive from them, and also some things you can't avoid. It's only when people are just biblical dabblers, dilettantes, that they find what they're looking for in the Bible. The trouble is, a great many of those who make a great noise about the Bible and its authority are precisely that: dilettantes and dabblers. They approach it as people approach a cafeteria, picking up the food that they like to eat, and without much concern for a balanced diet.

Question: I have to confess, it always jars me when I hear Christians quoting Karl Marx with approval. On several occasions in these meditations you have done that. In this one you referred to Marx's definition of religion as an opiate for the people ...

Response: Excuse me, but Marx didn't say religion was an opiate *for* the people. That's how Lenin formulated it. Marx said it was the opiate *of* the people. Lenin thought religion was laid on by the ruling classes to keep the people in their places. Marx was more subtle: he knew that people turn to religion themselves in order to avoid the pain of existence.

And I certainly think he was right. Half the religion on this continent today requires such an explanation. Some people get high on heroin, some on Jesus. This doesn't mean that I would agree with Marx that *all* religious faith is a matter of opting out. In fact, for me authentic faith, as distinct from religion, means just the opposite: opting *in*, deciding *for* the world, pain and all. But Christians need to become aware of the fact that all religion, including theirs, can be and frequently is used by human beings to escape from life. This may be harmless enough when it is indulged in by individual persons, but when it becomes a *public* phenomenon, with large numbers of people pursuing religion as a sort of sanctuary from the real problems of the world, it has vast political implications. When this happens, too, political forces that have their own interests at heart are easily able to take advantage of religion.

I don't know why so many Christians on this continent are threatened by Marxist insights of this nature, especially since the Bible had such insights thousands of years before Marx. Maybe it's because these insights hit so close to home. The odd thing is that while popular Christianity on our continent is so often anti-Marxist, most of the influential theologians of our century, Barth, Tillich and Niebuhr, to mention only three, have been deeply influenced by Marxist analysis. That by no means implies that they are Marxists. Nearly all 20th century theologians are critical of important aspects of Marx's thought. But it is strictly in line with the prophetic traditions of biblical faith to assume that God often speaks through voices outside the community of belief.

Question: Just a quick one: You made a fleeting reference to the word "prosperous," in its original sense, you said. I found it just a little strange that you seem to approve the desire for prosperity but on the other hand you've been critical all the way through of the search for success.

Response: That may be a little question, but it hides a very big distinction. Words are interesting, don't you think? Consider the word "prosperous" for a minute. The middle syllable, *sper*, comes from the Latin word *spes*, which means hope. (Incidentally, you may remember that in an earlier meditation I drew attention to the fact that this same Latin root is found in the English word "despair," the *de* simply meaning the absence of *spes* (spair). To long for prosperity means literally to live from hope, towards hope, in hope: to be *pro*-hope, so to speak. It has this future thrust. You haven't gotten there, but you are on the way.

Success on the other hand means you're there. You've made it! And that, in biblical perspective, is a very dangerous attitude, a delusion, in fact. Remember what St. Paul writes to the Corinthian church in I Corinthians 10: " . . . our fathers were all under the cloud, and all passed through the sea, and all were baptized into Moses . . . and all ate the same supernatural food . . . Nevertheless with most of them God was not pleased; for they were overthrown in the wilderness. . . . Therefore let any one who thinks that he stands take heed lest he fall."

Biblical faith when it reflects its Hebraic roots is not afraid to hope for prosperity, because matter is not evil and God intends us to enjoy this garden. But biblical faith is consistently skeptical about success, because it almost inevitably leads to delusions of grandeur and pompous behavior in relation to others. The rich man Dives in Jesus' parable (Luke 16:19 ff.) is finally just pathetic, for his wealth hides his real poverty as a human being. In the process, however, he is able to create a good deal of misery for poor Lazarus. The rich nations of the North today are pathetic too. How poor of spirit we are! But we are not just innocently pathetic, for we keep the poor peoples of the South poor, and threaten the peace of the whole world in order to retain our riches.

Question: You made another distinction that interested me, but I need to hear a little more about it. I mean when you said that many social changes (like food for the hungry and prison reforms and healing for the sick, all that sort of thing) are *possible*, though they are not *inevitable.* Would you kindly elaborate on that?

Response: The long answer to your question is Jürgen Moltmann's book, *The Theology of Hope.*[5] That's where I first learned this distinction myself. I think it is a very useful one. Christian hope means that we believe many things are *possible*, things that don't seem possible if your only basis for assessing their viability is past experience, precedent. Christians entertain the possibility of new things, because for them the grace of God means that God is always offering us a break with the past. The patterns, corporate as well as personal patterns by which we have governed, the ruts we have been running in—

these are not fixed, unchangeable; for God is "making all things new."

But this hope is not to be interpreted as if it were another way of speaking about good old American know-how and optimism. Optimism assumes that changes for the better are just built into the process. Progress is the character of time itself; and we New World societies are the cutting edge of progress. Christian hope rejects the optimistic assumption that everything is automatically getting better and better. Change for the better is always *possible*, but it is by no means *inevitable*. It is always possible that things will get worse, too.

There is in other words a condition that has to be met if we are to have life and not death. And that condition is that we shall *choose* the life, the "New Being" (Tillich), that God is graciously offering us. There is nothing inevitable here. Many things about our New World society today indicate our reluctance to make just such a choice. Perhaps in our disappointment about not being swept along automatically into ever expanding greatness, we are ready to capitulate too easily. We became so accustomed to the idea that we were simply destined to succeed that we find it hard to face the prospect that we may only find real life by engaging in a difficult struggle with failure.

That is why I have been writing and delivering these talks. I think that the Christian mission in our context today is to help people find sufficient wisdom and courage to believe that life is really possible. I mean authentic life, not just "our way of life." This is a very complicated task in many ways, because the people we are trying to help keep assuring themselves and one another at the rhetorical level that life is simply inevitable, while in the secret depths of their souls, as well as in their economic and other social patterns, they give every indication of having a hidden affair with death.

Our Christian mission in the affluent societies of the West, and particularly in North America, is much more difficult than is the mission of Third World Christians. I am talking, of course, about the spiritual-intellectual level. Third World peoples are oppressed peoples, and they know it. From the darkness of their situation they are ready to look for light; so that the Christian witness to the light of the gospel can have, in such situations, an immediate relevance. From the vantage-point of the impossible, one is ready to listen for the possible. But we affluent peoples of the North, who have been conditioned to regard our situation as brimful of possibilities and who can still seem to be in the limelight of history, are spiritually unprepared for the darkness that is today a global reality. We resist entertaining the impossibilities that we encounter, and we resist those who would bring us to a conscious awareness of these impossibilities; therefore we forfeit the real possibilities that are only open to those who have honestly confronted their limitations.

Question: Well, then, why don't Christians wait until people in our society can no longer indulge the luxury of hiding from themselves the limits they face? Why waste one's energy going about shouting that the house is on fire, when its inhabitants can still pretend that everything is in order?

Response: Because the truth is that we aren't living in a house, we're living in a tenement. We no doubt have the best unit in the place, and the fire can still seem a long way off. But it certainly won't be stopped by our flimsy fire-walls. And besides, the reason why it has got going so vigorously in the shabbier units of the tenement has a great deal to do with the way we have been living it up, our unconcern about the *whole* building, and our need to ignore fires.

AFTERWORD

I should like to close these reflections with a paragraph from the writings of the man to whom this volume is dedicated. He is a man who has not been given to extravagance of statement, who has manifested a unique fairness in respect to views that differ from his own, and also a loyal commitment to the democratic institutions of his country, the United States of America. It must therefore be taken with great seriousness when such a human being writes:

> I am still enough of a Christian realist to be inhibited about expecting profound changes of attitude in a nation as a whole, because there is a stubborn self-centeredness that easily gets moral support from ideas of national interest which in other contexts may be legitimate. But today the issues that we face are so grave, the simplest requirements of human concern for others are so clear, that a deep change in what people feel to be important to them and a real conversion of the mind and heart is called for. What is at stake overshadows the issues of the cold war that used to seem so important. Two things are at stake: the survival of a large part of humanity, and the humanity of those who survive because they live in privileged and protected countries.[1]

END NOTES

FIRST MEDITATION

[1]See my earlier publication, *The Reality of the Gospel and the Unreality of the Churches* (Philadelphia, The Westminster Press, 1975).

[2]Henry Pitney Van Dusen, *One Great Ground of Hope* (Philadelphia, The Westminster Press, 1961); p. 49.

[3]See Rosemary Ruether, *Faith and Fratricide* (New York, Seabury, 1974). See also *Antisemitism and the Foundations of Christianity*, Alan T. Davies, Ed. (New York, Paulist Press, 1979).

[4]See Paul Tillich, *The Protestant Era*, trans. by James Luther Adams, (Chicago, The University of Chicago Press, 1948), especially the discussion of "The Protestant Principle and the Proletarian Situation," pp. 161 ff. E.g. this: "What makes Protestantism Protestant is the fact that it transcends its own religious and confessional character, that it cannot be identified wholly with any of its particular historical forms." (p. 162)

[5]We do not have to strain to hear such affirmations. The largest Protestant denomination of this continent regularly insists that it is its Christian duty to convert the world to Christ "by the year 2,000" (the magical, millenial year); and our university campuses and TV screens are alive with the same sentiment.

[6]See Robert Lifton and Richard Falk, *Indefensible Weapons: The Political and Psychological Case Against Nuclearism* (Toronto C.B.C. Publications, 1982). Reference will be made to this study in the *Second Meditation*.

[7]Christopher Lasch, *The Culture of Narcissism: American Life in An Age of Diminishing Expectations* (New York, W.W. Norton & Co., Inc., 1978).

[8]It is hard to read of the courageous and dangerous undertakings of such organizations without feeling shamed. North American Christians need to be reminded today that the first victims of the Third Reich were not Christians but Communists and Socialists, who engaged in civil disobedience because they perceived the Nazi regime as an oppressive one. Fortunately some Christians—by no means the majority—in Germany joined them in protest. But it should give us pause to recall that, after the war, it was those who *obeyed* their structures of law and order who were called in question. As a recent article in *The Canadian Student* (Vol. 62, Nov. 1, 1983; p. 3) has stated it: "How many of us have ever considered that hundreds of Europeans were convicted in the Nuremburg trials of the 1940's because they refused to commit civil disobedience? The crimes of the Third Reich were all legal state activity, yet we are able to see that the planning and carrying out of genocide is a violation of all laws of morality. People had a responsibility to disobey the law. Is there not a strong parallel today, when weapons of mass destruction are increasingly available and governments openly contemplate their use? Civil

disobedience is the living witness that there are higher laws than those that our governments create or choose to enforce."

[9]An excellent example: "What is it About? Neither Superpower Can Explain a Competition that Threatens Mutual Annihilation," in *The Atlantic*, January, 1984; author, Thomas Powers.

[10](New York, Delacorte Press/Seymour Lawrence, 1979; p.xiii)

[11]I drew attention to this growing phenomenon in my book, *The Steward, op. cit.*

[12]The Protestant Reformers, Luther especially, distinguished between the "Church Visible" and the "Church Invisible." They did not mean that the real Church is literally invisible. But neither is it simply to be *equated* with the visible institutions called churches. There may be many within the churches who are Christians only in name; there may be many outside the structures of organized Christianity, also, who are true Christians. Tillich spoke of the latter as the "Latent Church."

[13]The Greek word *telos* can mean "end" in the sense of termination, and it can also mean the close or conclusion of anything; but the meaning that has dominated in Christian teleological discourse is the idea of *goal* and of the design or plan by which this goal might be reached. Hence one speaks of biblical faith as manifesting a *teleological view* of the universe, that is, a world view in which existence and history are purposeful, moving towards a meaningful end.

[14]The phrase is Paul Lehmann's. Prof. Lehmann makes this prevenient work of God in the world the presupposition of Christian ethics. It is the task of the church to discern where God is working in the world, and to participate in that work. (*Ethics in a Christian Context,* New York, Harper and Row, 1963.)

[15]For a lively and informed discussion of this phenomenon in the United States today see Jeremy Rifkin with Ted Howard, *The Emerging Order: God in the Age of Scarcity* (New York, G.P. Putnam's Sons, 1979).

[16]The term "ideology" can be used in a purely descriptive way to refer to the study or science (logos) of ideas. But it is frequently used as I am employing it here, i.e., to refer to the tendency to identify reality with one's *ideas* of reality, and thus to eliminate from one's conscious reflection the dimension of the unknown, the unpredictable, the contradictory, in short, the *mystery* of the world that is only partly accessible to our rational comprehension.

[17]The following statistics from the *World Christian Encyclopaedia* may be cited:
- "Between 1900 and 2000, classical Protestantism (in the U.S.A.) will have shrunk from two-thirds of the population to little more than one-third."
- "The most dramatic changes have been the rise for the first time of atheistic and nonreligious masses (now 20.8% of the world population as compared with .2% in 1900) and the precipitous decline of Chinese folk-religions and tribal faiths elsewhere."
- "After centuries as the predominant faith of the Northern Hemisphere, especially Europe, Christianity, as of 1981, had a nonwhite majority for the first time in 1200 years."
- In 1900 two-thirds of Christians lived in Europe and Russia; by 2000, three-fifths of them will live in Africa, Asia and Latin America. White Westerners cease to be practicing Christians at a rate of 7,600 per day."
- The (so-called) Evangelicals, taken all together, today command a healthy majority of Protestants in the world (157 millions) as well as in the U.S. (59 millions)."

These statements are taken from the "Religion" section of *Time Magazine*, May 3, 1982, No. 18; pp. 42–43, European Edition. *The World Christian Encyclopaedia* was edited by the Rev. Dr. David B. Barrett, and published in 1982 by the Oxford University Press. (See also the *Dialogue* after the *First Meditation*, pp. 39 ff.)

[18](New York, Avon, 1982; p. 188)

[19]*Systematic Theology*, Vol. III (Chicago, University of Chicago Press, 1963); p. 376.

[20]See *The Epistle to the Romans,* trans. by Edwyn C. Hoskyns (London, Oxford University Press, 1933, 1950).

[21]Edited by David B. Barrett (Oxford and New York, Oxford University Press, 1982). See especially the chapter: "Christianity in the Twentieth Century."

SECOND MEDITATION

[1]See Dorothy Sölle's book by this title (Philadelphia, Fortress Press, 1982).

[2](New York, The Viking Press, 1982); pp. 167–168.

[3](Harmondsworth, Penguin Books, 1978); pp. 410–411.

[4]*Op. cit.*

[5]*Cf. The Denial of Death* (New York, The Free Press, 1973); p. 178.

[6]A free translation of the 21st thesis of Luther's Heidelberg Disputation.

[7]Quoted by James Douglass in *The Non-Violent Cross: A Theology of Revolution and Peace* (New York, MacMillan Co., Inc., 1966); p. 257.

[8]*The Terminal Generation* (New York, Bantam Books, 1977); p. 188 ff.

[9]See *Sojourners*, Vol. 13, No. 8, September, 1984. Most of the articles in this pre-election issue are pertinent to the question under discussion.

[10]The familiar Jewish toast, "To Life!"

[11]Vol. 23, No. 8 (September, 1984); pp. 17 ff.

THIRD MEDITATION

[1]See for example the writings of Jacques Ellul, especially his perceptive study, *The Technological Society* (Alfred A. Knopf, Inc., 1964).

[2]*Polis*, from which we get our word "political," is the Greek word for city or city-state.

[3]"The Global Calling of American Christians," in *The Christian Century*, May 2, 1984; p. 458.

[4]An example of the creation of *Feindbilder*, taken at its most elementary, can be quoted from the Montreal *Gazette* (a daily newspaper) of February 18, 1984, describing the training of Canadian troops at Petawawa, Ontario. After a slide-

show depicting "the might of the Red Army," a sargeant tells the young re-
cruits, "many with peachfuzz moustaches waxed into baby handlebars": "The
Soviets do not take warfare as a joke. They put good men in and good equip-
ment to back them up . . . They are politically reliable. If they are told to shoot
their mothers, they shoot their mothers." Anyone who has seen (as I have)
the 16 to 18 year old Russian soldiers walking about the streets of Leipzig
or Prague looking utterly forlorn, lost and melancholy, would have a hard job
believing this rhetoric—even though he knows well enough that human beings will do dreadful things in a pinch, especially if it has been hammered into their teenage souls that "the enemy" will do dreadful things in a pinch.

[5]Trans. by Abott Justin McCann, Mentor Religious Classic, 1957; p. 17.

[6]In a television interview in 1975, Wiesel remarked that Christians seemed to
him too much interested in suffering and death. Another great Jewish sage,
the Canadian theologian Emil Fackenheim, once said to me (appropos of
nothing we were discussing): "I am against death." At the time I thought it
a strange statement. In retrospect it seems to me "of the essence" of biblical
faith, and a much-needed corrective to a certain type of Christian preoccupation with death.

[7]See *Letters and Papers from Prison*, (London, S.C.M. Press, 1971); pp. 336 ff.

[8](Toronto, McClelland and Stewart, first published in 1962; paperback edition
in New Canadian Library series [No. 82], 1972.)

[9]Published in 1978 by Editorial Orbe, Ciudad de la Habana, under the title (in
the English translation), "The Confession of Faith."

FOURTH MEDITATION

[1]*A Distant Mirror: The Calamitous Fourteenth Century* (New York, Alfred A.
Knopf, Inc., 1978).

[2](New York, W.W. Norton & Co., Inc., 1978.)

[3](San Francisco, W.H. Freeman & Co., 1970); p. 324.

[4]*The Nature and Destiny of Man*, Vol. II (New York, Charles Scribner's Sons,
1953); pp. 305, 306.

[5]*Ibid.*

[6]*Op. cit.*, p. 18.

[7](Philadelphia, Fortress Press, 1982.)

[8]*Theology of Culture*, (New York, Oxford University Press, 1959); p. 208.

[9](Philadelphia, Fortress Press, 1969.)

FIFTH MEDITATION

[1]*Mission and Grace: Essays in Pastoral Theology*, Vol. 1 (London, Sheed and
Ward, 1963); p. 84.

[2]*On Being a Christian*, trans. by Edward Quinn (Glasgow, Wm. Collins Sons and Co. Ltd., 1978); p. 571.

[3]Quoted from "The American Spirituality of Loren Eiseley" by Richard Wentz in *The Christian Century*, April 25, 1984; p. 432.

[4](New York, Washington Square Press, 1982); p. 178.

[5](New York, Harper and Row, 1967.)

AFTERWORD

[1]John C. Bennett, *The Radical Imperative: From Theology to Social Ethics*, (Philadelphia, The Westminster Press, 1975); p. 164.